MESSAGE OF BIBLICAL SPIRITUALITY

Editorial Director: Carolyn Osiek, RSCJ

Volume 4

Post-Exilic Prophets

Eileen Schuller, OSU

Michael Glazier
Wilmington, Delaware

About the Author

Eileen Schuller, OSU is presently Assistant Professor of Old Testament and Hebrew at Atlantic School of Theology, Halifax, Nova Scotia. She has studied at the University of Alberta, University of Toronto, Harvard University and in Jerusalem. Her main fields of interest have been the Post-Exilic period and Qumran.

First published in 1988 by Michael Glazier, Inc., 1935 West Fourth Street, Wilmington, Delaware 19805. ©1988 by Michael Glazier, Inc. All rights reserved.
Library of Congress Catalog Card Number: 88-81135.
International Standard Book Number:

    Message of Biblical Spirituality series: 0-89453-550-1, cloth;
                                    0-89453-566-8, paper.
    POST-EXILIC PROPHETS: 0-89453-554-4, cloth;
                         0-89453-570-6, paper.

Typography by Angela Meades. Cover design by Florence Bern. Printed in the United States of America.

TABLE OF CONTENTS

EDITOR'S PREFACE

One of the characteristics of church life today is a revived interest in spirituality. There is a growing list of resources in this area, yet the need for more is not exhausted. People are yearning for guidance in living an integrated life of faith in which belief, attitude, affections, prayer, and action form a cohesive unity which gives meaning to their lives.

The biblical tradition is a rich resource for the variety of ways in which people have heard God's call to live a life of faith and fidelity. In each of the biblical books we have a witness to the initiative of God in human history and to the attempts of people not so different from ourselves to respond to the revelation of God's love and care.

The fifteen volumes in the *Message of Biblical Spirituality* series aim to provide ready access to the treasury of biblical faith. Modern social science has made us aware of how the particular way in which one views reality conditions the ways in which one will interpret experience and life itself. Each volume in this series is an attempt to retell and interpret the biblical story from within the faith perspective that originally formed it. Each seeks to portray what it is like to see God, the world, and oneself from a particular point of view and to search for ways to respond faithfully to that vision. We who are citizens of our twentieth century world cannot be people of the ancient biblical world, but we can grow closer to their experience and their faith and thus closer to God, through the living Word of God which is the Bible.

The series includes an international group of authors representing England, Ireland, Canada, and the United States, but whose life experience has included first-hand knowledge of many other countries. All are proven scholars and committed believers whose faith is as important to them as their scholarship. Each acts as interpreter of one part of the biblical tradition in order to enable its spiritual vitality to be passed on to others. It is our hope that through their labor the reader will be able to enter more deeply into the life of faith, hope, and love through a fuller understanding of and appreciation for the biblical Word as handed down to us by God's faithful witnesses, the biblical authors themselves.

Carolyn Osiek, RSCJ
Associate Professor of New Testament Studies
Catholic Theological Union, Chicago

PREFACE

It might be helpful at the very beginning to say a few words of explanation about the intent and purpose of this book. Perhaps it is easier to say what it is not. This volume is not a commentary on individual books of the Old Testament prophets. Although specific prophetic passages are discussed, I do not want to give the impression that I have provided a complete and comprehensive exegesis of these texts; the reader will often want to consult a standard commentary (for example, from the Old Testament Message Series by Michael Glazier, Inc.,). Nor is this an academic work which consciously enters into dialogue or debate with other scholars. Any professionally trained persons who read these pages will immediately recognize my debt to much recent scholarly writing on the post-exilic prophets, and will also recognize where I have made specific choices between various approaches to the interpretation of the material (particularly with regard to such controversial issues as—to use standard scholarly terminology—the recrudescence of myth and the sociological matrix of the post-exilic community). However, I have not considered it the purpose of this book to enter into extended dialogue with the views of various scholars, nor necessarily to take the more academic methodological questions as my starting point.

As Carolyn Osiek has already indicated in the Editor's Preface, this book is an attempt to reflect upon a certain segment of the Old Testament, and to search out how it speaks, both to its original audience and to us today, of the mysterious working of our God. In these pages, we will attempt to enter into the world of the post-exilic prophets and to glimpse something of their unique experience of God. In some ways, this task is rendered more difficult because our particular corpus of material is often less familiar to the reader than other parts of the Old Testament. Thus, a certain amount of attention (particularly in the first two chapters) has been devoted to situating the prophets within their historical context and to providing a brief overview and outline of their message and concerns. I hope that the reader who is more concerned with the spiritual aspects of the prophets will not be discouraged, nor too readily dismiss these chapters; often reflection on what seem to be more academic and historical questions can lead to valuable new insights and theological understanding.

If these prophets do not speak in a historical vacuum, neither do we hear them in a vacuum. Even the most basic decisions which I have had to make in the course of writing (such as the choice of specific passages to be discussed and the organization of the material into some coherent form) are influenced not only by what the prophets said some twenty-five centuries ago, but also by the concerns of the twentieth century. Anyone who looks at the Table of Contents will note that the topics discussed are, to some extent, those which awaken our imagination today (concerns with the issues of language and the naming of God, with social justice, with the future); doubtless too, my own personal agenda, my prejudices and idiosyncracies have entered into the format. While I have tried to be sensitive and alert to what seem to be the dominant concerns of these prophets, it is important to acknowledge that what is written here is an interpretation—as, in fact, all spirituality must be. These pages are meant to open a door; hopefully the readers, having made that first initial step, will be empowered to continue their own exploration.

Throughout the writing of this book, I have been at times fascinated and at time paralyzed by the wealth of the biblical material with which I am dealing. As I finish the book, I am profoundly aware that what I have written is only a beginning. It is only *one* of many possible approaches to the richness of the prophetic message. I take heart in recalling the words of Père Roland de Vaux, the great Dominican archaeologist and scholar; lecturing at Harvard University in 1976, he commented, "What I know today, I teach today. What I will know tomorrow, I will teach tomorrow." Both for the reader and for myself the search is on-going and continuous as we attempt to discern something of the mysterious divine self-disclosure in the words of the prophets. The very incompleteness of our fragile efforts is not a cause for discouragement, but a concrete recognition of the power of God's Word; we are renewed in our efforts by the promise concerning this Word

> It shall not return to me empty,
> but it shall accomplish that which I purpose,
>> and prosper in the thing for which I sent it (Isa 55:11).

The biblical quotations throughout this book are all taken from the Revised Standard Version (RSV) unless otherwise indicated, with only slight changes to the modern form of the second person. In the end, it seemed better to keep to a standard biblical translation in spite of the problems created by the non-inclusivity of the language.

No book is ever written without the help, either direct or indirect, of many people. I would like to thank in a special way Carolyn Osiek, the editor of this series, who asked me to write this volume; I am grateful for her patient guidance of a novice writer and for her unwavering conviction that indeed— someday—a book would be forthcoming. Both the readability and the clarity of this volume have been enhanced by the careful attention given it by my student and friend, Janis Anderson. In a particular way, I want to thank all the students of the Atlantic School of Theology, who have patiently explored with me many of the topics in this book in various courses over the last five years; more than they perhaps realize, I have learned so much from their questions and discussions. Atlantic School of Theology is a unique institution, a single theological school which prepares candidates for ordained and lay ministry in the Roman Catholic, Anglican and United Church of Canada; in both the joys and the struggles of living ecumenically together day-by-day, we are learning something of what it means to "dream dreams and . . . see visions" (Joel 2:28).

This book is dedicated to my father, Norbert, a man among those who "rely upon their hands and are skillful in their own work . . . they keep stable the fabric of the world, and their prayer is in the practice of their trade" (Sir 38:31, 34).

1

GENERAL INTRODUCTION

"How shall we sing the Lord's song in a foreign land?" (Ps 137:4). This was the plaintive cry voiced by a people who found themselves exiles in a foreign land; this was the lament and question of a conquered people who had suddenly lost freedom, land, king and Temple, and in that catastrophe, experienced the loss of their God.

The event which we call "the Exile" was a traumatic experience, a time of crisis for the people of God. This was the people to whom the Lord had promised "I will take you for my people, and I will be your God (Ex 6:7)." They had been delivered "with a mighty hand and an outstretched arm" from slavery and oppression in Egypt to freedom in the land promised to their ancestors. Through Moses on Mount Sinai they had received the Law of the Lord (the Torah) instructing them how to live their lives in response to the covenant which God had initiated. In time, the Lord had chosen for them a king, David, and given the assurance "your house and your kingdom shall be made sure forever before me; your throne shall be established forever" (2 Sam 7:16). Over the centuries, the prophets had spoken to them the Word of God in judgement and in promise. Then, suddenly, in the year 587 B.C. all was called into question when the mighty Babylonian

Empire conquered the tiny and vulnerable kingdom of Judah. Many of the people, especially the leaders and the elite, were carried off to the foreign land of Babylon as exiles; the Temple, the sacred site of divine presence, was burned; King Zedekiah was blinded and taken way in fetters. What kind of God could do this, or even allow such ignominy to befall the people who had been chosen to be "a kingdom of priests and a holy nation" (Ex 19:6)? Was it perhaps that this God, who centuries earlier had revealed the divine name as YHWH (the Lord), was this God one who would turn and destroy his own people? Was it that Marduk, the god of the Babylonian conquerors, had shown himself more powerful? Perhaps the lesson to be learned from these events was that Marduk, not the Lord, was to be worshipped and adored.

Like the Exodus, the Exile was a turning point in God's relationship with the chosen people. On the surface, it looked as if the kingdom of Judah might disappear as totally as the ten lost tribes of the northern Kingdom had vanished a century earlier. However, in spite of the tremendous suffering involved and the profound crisis of faith engendered, this was ultimately to be not a time of destruction but of reconstruction. It became a time for the reexamination of old traditions and the discovery of new, hitherto unimagined ways of being God's people. Through the whole Exile experience, it was the prophets (Jeremiah, Ezekiel, Second Isaiah) who spoke a new message of hope in the midst of hopelessness.

After some fifty years or so (587-539 BC), the people finally did return to their land and slowly they began the tedious task of rebuilding and restoration. Though the Temple was rededicated in 515 BC, the land still remained under the control of Persia, with a governor and high priest exercising authority over this small province. In 313 BC, the Greek armies under Alexander the Great conquered the Persians and became the ruling power in Palestine until the Roman conquest in 60 BC. But over all these centuries, whoever was the current ruling power, little changed for the Jewish community in Palestine. These were centuries of poverty and struggle. Judah was no longer a major power on the map of world history; as Ezra acknowledged in his prayer "We are bondmen" (Ezra 9:9). Our sources of information are scattered and limited; there is simply much that we do not know even about major events during these centuries. In the words of the prophet Zechariah, this was indeed "the day of small things" (Zech 4:10). In the next chapter, we will be looking in somewhat greater depth at what was happening in this period and how the voice of prophecy continued to be heard for a time and then faded.

Exile Now

This harsh and little known period of biblical history does not belong only to the past. It both corresponds with and has something to say to much in our present day experience, both of our culture and of our faith.

Many people today know, in a real and concrete way, what it means literally to be in exile, to be away from home and homeland. On an unprecedented scale, in every one of our cities and even in our towns and villages, we meet refugees thousands of miles from their real homeland—men, women and children who have been forced into exile by economic oppression or violent political regimes. Others, the street men and shopping-bag ladies, young and old, who inceasingly walk the streets of our cities experience a different but equally terrifying exile from the stability of home and fixed address. In still another sense, the Russian Jews, the "refusniks," who are denied permission to emigrate vividly describe their situation as an exile from their own state.

But, "one can be in exile without ever leaving the land."[1] The experience of geographical exile is a rich and resilient paradigm for a complex set of experiences of loss, rejection and new beginnings. The metaphor of exile, at least as it arises out of the biblical paradigm, involves a threefold dynamic: upheaval and loss of what was; the disorientation and uncertainty of a new and temporary existence cut off from traditional support systems; and the hope and vision of a restoration which, while related in some way to the old, must be radically new. In today's society, exile comes in a variety of guises. For many, the future seems not a logical unfolding of the present but a strange and foreign land overrun with problems and questions which defy not only solution but even definition and analysis. One need only mention the issues of world hunger, the proliferation of nuclear weapons, the threats to the environment; it is as if we are exiled from our very hopes and dreams. On a more personal level, exile can be known in the experience of unemployment, in the breakdown of a marriage, in prolonged and crippling illness, in the loneliness of old age. Recently, to give just one current example, Baptist women clergy who have been denied recognition by their own Southern Baptist Convention took up this image to articulate their sense of loss and betrayal, "In many ways we feel like exiles."[2]

[1]Ralph Klein, *Israel in Exile*, (Fortress Press, 1979), p. 149. The entire chapter "Light for our Exile," pp 149-154, is a perceptive reflection on how we experience exile in our society and individual lives today.

[2]Susan Lockwood Wright, "SBC Women Ministers Break Their Silence," *Christian Century*, November 12, 1986, p. 999.

More and more, there is a sense today that, in a world in which Christianity is not the primary force either in terms of sheer numbers or of moral and spiritual persuasion, the simple fact of professing faith in Jesus Christ makes us "strangers and exiles on the earth" (Heb 11:13).

In much of contemporary Christian reflection about the Old Testament, it is the Exodus which emerges as the focal and starting point for reflection, the paradigm for understanding not only what happened then but also what is happening to us now. The mighty act of God in delivering a people from slavery to freedom functions as the pivotal event in the faith of Israel, the fundamental datum in interpreting history, creation and salvation. The choice of Exodus as the dominant biblical image is particularly characteristic of that theological approach which is broadly identified as Liberation Theology. Many examples could be quoted: Reuben Alves calls the Exodus "the paradigm for the interpretation of all space and all time";[3] J. Severino Croatto claims that "the Exodus becomes an inexhaustible reservoir-of-meaning." [4] Yet, I want to suggest that Exile, rather than Exodus, might be a hermeneutical key which will enable us to explore certain aspects of the contemporary situation in the light of biblical witness. Above all, it is the lived experience of exile, whether geographical or metaphorical, which forces us to confront some of the most disturbing and profound questions about the reliability of the divine promise and the meaning of suffering.

[3]Quoted and translated by E. Dussel, "Exodus as a Paradigm in Liberation Theology," in *Exodus: A Lasting Paradigm*, eds. B. van Iersel and A. Weiler, Concilium 189, (T & T Clark, 1987), p. 94.

[4]J. Severino Croatto, *Exodus: A Hermeneutics of Freedom*, Orbis Books, (Maryknoll, 1981), p. 13.

Exodus-faith calls forth one dynamic and one type of response, but it is the experience of exile which calls forth a new depth of faith. In a very perceptive essay a few years back, Douglas Hall laments that:

> To entertain the negative (the Night!) by which we are actually engulfed today is a spiritual feat of which most North Americans are simply not capable. We have no frame of reference, no *mythos*, for the experience of negation.[5]

Sustained reflection on the exile experience of Israel might help us to name and recognize our own exile, both personal and communal, and give us a paradigm and a vocabulary to talk about those aspects of our reality which so much of contemporary culture tries so desperately to deny and dismiss. And, if "the zero hour breeds new algebras" (to use the words of the poet Amos Wilder,[6]) we may also discover in the very experience of exile the beginnings of a new hope.

The Study of the Post-Exilic Period

Throughout this book, we will be examining and reflecting upon some of the less well known sections of the Bible. Most people have some general acquaintance with the foundational stories of the Old Testament: the creation stories (Gen 1-3), the call of Abraham (Gen 12, 15), the deliverance through the Red Sea (Ex 1-15), the giving of the Law to Moses on Mount Sinai (Ex 19-24), the choice of David as king (2 Sam 7). Each

[5]Douglas John Hall, "Towards an Indigenous Theology of the Cross," *Interpretation*, 30, 1976, p. 158.

[6]Amos Wilder, "A hard Death," *Poetry*, 107, 1965-1966, pp 168-169.

year at Christmas, either in the readings of the liturgy, or by listening to Handel's Messiah, we hear again the much-loved passages linked to the promise of a Messiah, "For to us a child is born, to us a son is given" (Isa 9:6); "a young woman shall conceive and bear a son" (Isa 7:14). Especially in the last years, there has been tremendous interest in the words of the prophets which proclaim the message of God's concern for the poor and the obligations of social justice. Certain texts have become classic: "What does the Lord require of you but to do justice" (Mic 6:8); "Let justice roll down like waters, and righteousness like an ever-flowing stream" (Amos 5:24); "They shall beat their swords into plowshares, their spears into pruning hooks" (Isa 2:4).

But who today reads Haggai? Or Zechariah? Or Malachi? Or Chronicles? Many people would even have somewhat of a problem to find these books in their Bible! Yet, they are there. They are part of God's word to us, accepted into the canon of received Scripture. It is precisely these books which will be the focus of this volume.

Before concentrating specifically on the later prophets, I want to digress for a moment and reflect more specifically on the issue just raised: why are certain books or certain sections of the Bible often relatively unknown to us? Why, in fact, do we often act as if the Bible were concerned with events from the Exodus down through Jeremiah or so, and then picked up again with the coming of Jesus? I would like to suggest three reasons for our selective reading.

(1) The Way We Learn Scripture

In some cases, I think that the reason is simply pragmatic. Many people, lay and religious, as well as priests trained in a seminary situation, have at some time taken formal courses in Old and New Testament. In most academic situations, such courses are taught over a single term. I know that when I teach an Introduction to the Old Testament, there is just so much material and so little time that we are lucky to trace developments down to prophets like Jeremiah or Ezekiel and the Exile. Often, in the very last class of the term, I am making a breathless dash to get the Chosen People back from Babylon to their own land, and, with perhaps time for a few moments on the book of Daniel, the term is over. Usually the students will take a course the next semester on the New Testament which will begin with the birth of Jesus, with perhaps an introductory lecture giving a quick survey of the historical situation in the Greco-Roman world. As a result, the whole period from 600 BC to the beginning of the first century AD remains largely a blur and the impression is given that nothing much of importance happened then. Furthermore, if this has been a person's training as a priest or religious educator, one will probably not jump at the chance to preach or lead a bible study on Haggai!

(2) *The Influence of the Lectionary*

A second reason why much of the material in these Old Testament books is unknown to most Catholics is that these texts do not figure prominently in the Sunday readings as prescribed in the Lectionary. On the one hand, following St. Jerome's warning that "ignorance of the Scriptures is ignorance of Christ," in recent years there has been tremendous importance placed on the daily devotional reading of the Scriptures. Yet, in reality, for many Catholics, their principal access to the bible is through the readings at Sunday Mass; in a very real sense, this becomes "the Bible" for them. Thus, for instance, prior to Vatican II, Catholics were primarily familiar with Matthew's Gospel and with a relatively limited number of Epistle texts read in a one-year cycle. After 1969, many more biblical passages were included in the three-year Lectionary cycle both in the Catholic tradition and in other churches such as Anglican, Lutheran, and Methodist which adopted some variation of the Roman Lectionary.

Even a cursory examination of the Roman Lectionary reveals that over the three-year-cycle the congregation hears rather extensive segments from Second Isaiah and Third Isaiah (especially in the Advent-Christmas season, and such key passages as the Suffering Servant Songs on Palm Sunday and Good Friday), two passages from Malachi, two from Zechariah, and perhaps one from Joel on Ash Wednesday. No passages are read from Haggai, the first eight chapters of Zechariah, or Obadiah. Churches which use the Common Lectionary (as proposed by the Consultation on Common Texts) would hear one passage from Haggai, a more representative passage from Zechariah, and an additional selection from Joel and Malachi. Thus, there is exposure only to a limited amount of material. Furthermore, according to the principles on which the Roman Lectionary is based, for most of the church year the Old Testament reading is selected so that it relates in some way to the Gospel passage. For example, two passages are chosen from Zechariah (Zech 12:10-11 "when they look on him whom they have pierced" and Zech 9:9-10 "your king . . . humble and riding on an ass") because these traditionally have been interpreted in a christological sense; yet, these selections do not necessarily capture the main thrust of the prophet's message. Thus, it is often difficult "to get a feel" of the post-exilic prophets, their perspectives and concerns, solely from the Lectionary selections. This is not so much a criticism as the recognition of a fact, which partially explains why these later prophets are often so unfamiliar to us.

(3) Our Understanding of the Development of Judaism

There is still another reason why we pay so little attention to the post-exilic period, a reason which is much more serious. Often, consciously or unconsciously, this goes back to how we understand God's self-revelation in word and in deed. In biblical scholarship, there was a certain theoretical understanding which developed throughout the nineteenth century, a certain basic conceptual framework for viewing biblical history and religion. In many ways, this construct was given its classical expression by the German scholar Julius Wellhausen in a famous book *Prolegomena to the History of Ancient Israel* (1885). Although few, if any, scholars today would agree with Wellhausen completely, some of the effects of his theory live on—though, interestingly, more in popular works on the bible or in Sunday homilies than in serious scholarly works. Put simply, this approach, influenced by certain nineteenth century philosophical trends, claimed that Israelite religion followed an evolutionary pattern. It began with the simple primitive animism of the Mosaic period. Then, in the eighth century BC came the prophets—religious radicals, rugged individualists pitted against "the establishment," particularly against formal cultic religious ritual. As the result of personal mystical religious experience the prophets brought to expression, for the first time, the purest of ethical and spiritual development. Subsequent history had nowhere to go but down! Thus, the post-exilic period was viewed as a degradation of the "pure ethical monotheism" of the prophets, corrupted by the introduction of the vast legal sections of the Bible.

Religion was, in these centuries, reduced to a codification and canonization of ethical and ritualistic law. A "church" or theocracy was born which we now call "Judaism," a religious entity radically different from the world inhabited by Moses and the prophets; indeed, for Wellhausen, it was a disposable entity, "Judaism is a mere empty chasm over which one springs from the Old Testament to the New."[7] Thus, Jesus and his message (at least before it too was corrupted by the Christian church) stands as a radical protest against, and the antithesis of, the legalism and formalism of Judaism.

I have described this Wellhausenian view at some length, not because I agree with it, but because its influence is still much with us. This is not just an abstract scholarly theory, but a way of thinking which has had far-reaching and even frightening ramifications. Obviously, if this is our understanding of how we come to know God's revelation, there is little need to devote much time and effort to the post-exilic period. The assumption is that it has little or nothing to teach us except perhaps by way of negative example—better to concentrate on important things like Moses and the early prophets. Furthermore, such a conceptualization shapes how we understand the living religion of Judaism, for in many respects, religious Jews today see themselves as the direct descendants of Judaism as it developed in the post-exilic period. If Judaism is deficient in its very origins, if its leaders like Ezra (who is revered in Judaism as "a second Moses") are only narrow-minded legalists, this attitude cannot help but affect how we view and how we treat the present day living descendants of the post-exilic period.

[7]Julius Wellhausen, *Prolegomena to the History of Ancient Israel*, (Adam & Charles Black, 1885), p. 1.

Prophecy In The Post-Exilic Period

In this book, we are going to be focusing specifically on the prophets who were active during the actual time of the Exile, in the immediate years of the return to Palestine, and throughout the subsequent centuries. However, the prophets were only *one* group in the new society which was taking shape in response to the crisis of exile. In fact, as we will see in a moment, both the role of the prophet and the nature of prophetic influence were in a state of radical flux. In the years immediately preceding the Exile, when the prophet Jeremiah outlined the three dominant leadership groups (18:18), he singled out

> the priests—who give instruction (Torah)
> the wise—who speak counsel
> the prophets—who announce the Word.

In the post-exilic period, the role of the priest expanded both in scope and in influence; indeed, the Restoration community as reflected in the book of Chronicles can be described as a theocracy in which priests and Temple played a dominant role, even in the political and economic spheres. When the Torah, as a written document, became the constitutional and legal foundation of the community, the wise, "the Sages" as they are called in later Jewish tradition, came to occupy a central position with their emphasis on learning, teaching and the interpretation of the law. Thus, while our focus will be on the prophets, they can only properly be understood within the context of religious and sociological development as a whole.

However, even with regards to the prophets, this book consciously plunges *in medias res*. It is meant to be read in close conjunction with the other volume in this Message of Biblical

Spirituality Series, *Pre-Exilic Prophecy* by Bishop Richard J. Sklba. There you will find a fuller treatment of such fundamental topics as "What is a prophet?," "How did prophecy begin?," "How did the first prophets speak and act?" Bishop Sklba describes the history and message of the prophets from the ninth to the sixth century; I refer you to his book for a discussion of these questions, and will not attempt to duplicate them here, except where they arise naturally within our examination of specific prophetic texts.

If, as we have just discussed, the post-exilic period in general has not always fared well in terms of our appreciation of its importance, the same can be said even more forcibly with regard to the study of prophecy in this period. Many older works tended to assume that prophecy ended abruptly at the Exile, or at least any really significant or "great" prophecy. For instance, there is the old but much-quoted statement of A.B. Davidson in reference to the prophet Jeremiah, "Prophecy had already taught its truth, its last effort was to reveal itself in a life."[8] Or, to quote D. Winton Thomas, "He [Deutero-Isaiah] is the last of the great Old Testament prophets."[9] Often the comment is made that the later prophets no longer dealt with the vital themes of classical prophecy, but rather treated "merely Jewish concerns"—temple, priesthood, sacrifice, fasting.

Such an approach bespeaks an understanding which is more or less consciously simplistic. It presumes that pre-exilic prophecy is the "Golden Age," the pinnacle of religious development, and whatever is different in subsequent ages is,

[8]J. Hastings, *Dictionary of the Bible*, II, (T. & T. Clark, 1899), p. 576.

[9]D. Winton Thomas, "The Sixth Century B.C.: A Creative Epoch in the History of Israel," *Journal of Semitic Studies*, 6, 1961, p. 39.

by definition, a sign of decline to the "Silver Age." As a fundamental beginning premise, I would like to suggest that change can also indicate vitality and life: it is precisely because these later prophets were unlike the earlier prophets that they were able to continue to speak God's Word in radically altered circumstances.

The Prophetic Corpus

If the view that prophecy simply died or petered out at the Exile were the whole truth, this would be a short volume indeed! At the risk of belaboring the obvious, it is worthwhile just to point out that, of the fifteen books in the prophetic corpus, five are clearly post-exilic:

Haggai
Zechariah
Joel
Malachi
Jonah

Furthermore, the prophets Jeremiah and Ezekiel proclaimed their message throughout the crucial years leading up to the destruction of Jerusalem and the early years of Exile, Jeremiah living in Palestine and Egypt, and Ezekiel in Babylon. The shortest book of the Old Testament, the prophecy of Obadiah, clearly is speaking of conditions at the time of the Exile. One major section of the book of Isaiah, chapters 40-55, comes from an unnamed prophet (commonly referred to as Second Isaiah or Deutero-Isaiah) who lived during the Exile in Babylon. The final section of the book of Isaiah, chapters 56-66, comes from a prophet or a series of prophets (in any case, called Third

Isaiah or Tritero-Isaiah) who were active in the years following the return to Palestine. In addition, there are certainly small sections within other prophetic collections which scholars suggest (on the basis of content and form) belong to the post-exilic period. This means that almost all the prophetic books as we have them today are the result of a development over centuries of time; the words of prophets such as Amos and Hosea were continually updated and reread in a new way so that they could still function as the Word of God to later generations. Although it is often difficult to be totally certain of dates, most scholars would place in the post-exilic period such passages as Isa 24-27 (the Isaiah Apocalypse), Ezek 38-39, Isa 2:1-4 (a passage also found in Mic 4:1-5), many of the prose sections in the book of Jeremiah, and numerous other short units. So, all in all, this is a substantial corpus of material; the problems in understanding post-exilic prophecy cannot be reduced to pleading a shortage of material!

Let me say something about the specific limits (most of them self-imposed) as to the texts to be considered in this volume. Our discussion will focus on the prophets Second Isaiah, Third Isaiah, Haggai, Zechariah, Malachi, and Joel. The two major prophets, Jeremiah and Ezekiel, are certainly relevant in that they both began their ministry before the Exile and continued to preach after the events of 587 BC (for further discussion, see pp. 40-44). But because, in so many ways, these two prophets belong more to the pre-exilic era, I will not be treating them in any comprehensive way in this volume, although many references will be made to their words. Furthermore, the book of Jonah will not be treated here, simply because it is dealt with elsewhere in this series in Volume 7, *The Old Testament Short Story: Explorations into Narrative Spirituality* by Carmel McCarthy and William Riley. Finally, mention should be made of the book of Baruch which is found in Catholic Bibles among the prophetic books (after Jeremiah and Lamentations and before Ezekiel); in Protestant Bibles, this is one of the seven books which is either omitted or included in the special section of the Apocrypha. Although the opening verses identify the book as the words of the scroll written by Baruch, the scribe of Jeremiah (Jer 32:12) in the fifth year of the Babylonian Exile (582 BC), the material is certainly from much later. These chapters are a diverse collection: prayers of penitence, a hymn in praise of Wisdom, a poem about Jerusalem, and a letter against idolatry. The book of Baruch is so distinctive from the other prophetic works which we are considering that it will not be treated in this volume;   it really belongs with other more wisdom-like collections.

In our listing of post-exilic prophets above perhaps you noted that the book of Daniel is not included. Yet, if you look at most standard English Bibles, you will see Daniel among the prophetic books (after Ezekiel and before Hosea). Furthermore, the events in which Daniel participates are precisely dated to the exilic and early post-exilic period (from the "third year of the reign of Jehoiachim" Dan 1:1, 606 BC, to the reign of Darius 522 BC). There are certain texts in both Jewish and Christian sources which clearly call Daniel a prophet, for example, Matt 24:15 "So when you see the desolating sacrilege spoken of by the prophet Daniel"; and a text from Qumran (4QFlorilegium 1-3 ii 3) where a time of affliction is predicted "as it is written in the book of Daniel the prophet." Yet, in the earliest Hebrew manuscripts, the book of Daniel comes, not after Ezekiel, but in the third part of the Scripture, "the Writings," between Esther and Ezra (and this is where it is found today in the modern Bibles published by the Jewish

Publication Society).

In many ways, Daniel is very unlike any of the other prophetic books. The long visions with their bizarre images, the angelic figure which mediates divine revelation, the cosmic upheavals, the cryptic use of numbers—all these are unparalleled in even the latest prophetic books. Furthermore, in the book itself, Daniel is described as wise (Dan 1:3-5, 2:48-49) but not as a prophet, and he never employs the distinctive prophetic formula "Thus says the Lord." Furthermore, modern scholarship has shown that the book of Daniel was composed in the years 167-164 BC during the heart of the Maccabean crisis; that is, considerably later than any of our other prophetic books and right at the time when the author of 1 Maccabees tells us that there was no prophet to be found in the land (see p. 32). The book of Daniel can best be understood when we recognize that it is not, strictly speaking, prophecy at all. Rather, chapters 7-12 belong to a different genre of literature technically called "apocalyptic," a distinctive (and often difficult) way of writing which must be interpreted in a distinctive manner if it is to yield up its treasure of meaning. Thus, although apocalyptic shares certain features with prophecy (for instance, a concern for the future and for God's action in history), it is a separate type of literature which we will not be able to consider within the confines of this volume.[10]

Other Prophets?

Do these prophetic books which we have just listed give us a complete picture of prophetic activity in this period? Or,

---

[10]The reader is referred to Volume 15 of the Message of Biblical Spirituality Series, *The Apocalypse of John*, by Seán P. Kealy, for an introduction to apocalyptic thought in general and to the Apocalypse of John.

were there still other prophets whose words have not been preserved and collected for us in a book? Actually, there are a surprising number of different references to what someone has called "the unpublished prophets," some of whom we know by name, and some of whom just appear as "the prophets."

The last days of the kingdom of Judah were a time of vibrant prophetic activity. For instance, when King Josiah discovered the book of the Law during his repair of the Temple, it was to the prophetess Huldah that he turned to have it authenticated (2 Kgs 22:14). In the tumultuous world of international politics when decisions had to be made about showing allegiance, resisting or collaborating, various prophets gave conflicting messages, but all claimed to speak in the name of the Lord. Jeremiah at time speaks with great bitterness of those prophets who claim to have stood in the Council of the Lord, when in fact they are simply speaking their own word (Jer 23:16-40). His conflict with the prophet Hananiah over whether the Lord's word is one of peace or one of war is vividly described in chapter 28. We hear of another prophet Uriah, who "prophesied against this city and against this land in words like those of Jeremiah" (Jer 26:20), and was put to death by King Jehoiachim. Certain of the prophets seem to have gone to Babylon with the first groups of exiles—we know that Ezekiel was part of the deportation of 593 BC. In his letter to the exiles, Jeremiah warns them not to listen to "your prophets and your diviners who are among you" (Jer 29:8), prophets who were apparently preaching a message of immediate deliverance.

Although Haggai and Zechariah are the two prophets mentioned by name at the time of the Restoration, a few texts speak of "the prophets" as if there were more (Zech 7:3, 8:9, Ezra 5:2). Later, in the days of the governor Nehemiah (circa

450 BC), Sanballat accused Nehemiah of churning up prophetic support, "and you have also set up prophets to proclaim concerning you in Jerusalem 'There is a king in Judah' " (Neh 6:7); there is mention of a prophet Shemaiah (Neh 6:10), a prophetess Noadiah, and "the rest of the prophets who wanted to make me afraid" (Neh 6:14).

Most of the other references to prophets and prophetic activity in the post-exilic period come from the two books of Chronicles (a priestly retelling of Israel's history, probably written around 500 BC but redacted and revised throughout the next century). The author of Chronicles frequently designates as "prophets" the Levitical temple singers in the days of King David who "prophesy with lyres, with harps and with cymbals" (1 Chr 25:1, 2 Chr 29:25). Although the Chronicler is describing the First Temple period, he is retrojecting back into pre-exilic times his particular priestly understanding, namely that the composition and rendition of liturgical music was a form of prophecy. In a later Jewish text, David, the originator of temple music, is said to have composed over four thousand psalms and songs "through prophecy which was given him from before the Most High" (11QPs^a xxvii 11; note also Acts 2:30). Thus, in the priestly worldview, prophecy was radically reinterpreted and absorbed into the cult.

The End Of Prophecy

Sometime in the period after the fifth century, prophecy as an institution ceased to exist. There is so much that we simply do not know about the historical process, the dates, and the reasons. The latest collections of prophetic material are all notoriously difficult to fit into any concrete historical context, (we will take this up in somewhat more detail in the next chapter). Though some of the material certainly comes from the fifth century (Joel, Malachi), there is little which can be placed in the fourth or third centuries with any degree of certainty. But, exactly when or why prophecy "died" is a mystery shrouded in the shadows of time.

After a long period of silence, a few rays of light appear in the second century BC, but only to reveal that prophecy is no longer a living and functioning institution. After his victory in 164 BC, Judas Maccabeus had to determine what to do with the altar which had been profaned by the Greek king Antiochus Epiphanes, "So they tore down the altar, and stored the stones in a convenient place on the temple hill until there should come a prophet to tell them what to do with them" (1 Mac 4:45-46). Implicit in this statement is the acknowledgement that such a prophet was not now to be found (note also 1 Mac 14:41, Simon is to be king "until a trustworthy prophet should arise"). In 1 Mac 9:27, in a more or less passing comment on the havoc wrought at the Battle of Berea we read, "Thus there was great distress in Israel, such as had not been since the time that the prophets ceased to appear among them." A number of later non-biblical texts evince this same assumption that "the spirit of prophecy had left Israel" as later Talmudic texts phrase it (b. San 11a; b. Yoma 96b; b. Sotah 48b). The historian Josephus, writing in the first century AD, also limited the age of prophecy to the period between Moses and Artaxerxes (probably meaning here Artaxerxes I who died in 424 BC). Later Jewish tradition which saw the sages (that is, the rabbis) as the religious leaders described the transition as follows: "Since the days when the Temple was destroyed, prophecy has been taken from the prophets and given to the wise" (b.BB 12a).

But why did prophecy disappear at a certain period in the history of God's people? There is certainly no one simple answer to this question. Perhaps by the time we come to the end of our study, you may have a few suggestions of your own as explanation. For the present, let me suggest three factors which we can keep in mind as we work with this material.

(1) In the first place, prophecy contains within itself an innate fragility and vulnerability. The prophet speaks as a messenger, "Thus says the Lord"; he or she claims to have stood in the Council of the Lord (Jer 23:18-22) to hear the divine decrees which are to be communicated to the people. Once the prophet has experienced the Lord, the prophet is compelled to speak, "Woe to me, but that I speak, it was like a fire burning within me" (Jer 5:14, 23:28-29). But who can authenticate that claim? What outside authority can prove that this is a genuine spiritual experience and not simply self-delusion? We ask these same questions today when we have people in our christian community, or prayer groups, or families, who confidently claim "the Lord told me" or "the Lord told me to tell you to do such and such." We know how difficult and painful it is to judge the authenticity of such experiences.

This question—which is often expressed in terms of true prophet versus false prophet[11]—became especially crucial during the final days before the Exile. As we have already noted, it came to a head in the conflict between the prophet Hananiah who claimed that the Lord was speaking a word of peace "Thus says the Lord of hosts, the God of Israel, I have broken the yoke of the king of Babylon" (Jer 28:2), and

---

[11]For a helpful study of the way in which prophetic conflict contributed to the demise of prophecy, see J. Crenshaw, *Prophetic Conflict: Its Effect on Israelite Religion*, BZAW 124, (De Gruyter, 1971).

Jeremiah who claimed "Thus says the Lord of hosts, the God of Israel: I have put upon the neck of all these nations an iron yoke of the servitude to Nebuchadnezzar king of Babylon and they shall serve him" (Jer 28:14). To us, with hindsight, who know the outcome of history, the decision as to which is the true prophet seems blatant and clear; we are quite ready to be suspicious of "the prophet who prophesies peace" (Jer 28:9). But, a few years later, another prophet would come proclaiming peace, "Comfort, comfort my people" (Isa 40:1) and he was to be recognized as a true prophet!

(2) This leads us to the second point. Although we often tend to think of the prophets as rugged individualists and anti-establishment figures, prophecy is, by definition, a social institution. A great deal of recent writing on biblical prophecy has focused on the conditions which are needed in a society before prophecy can function and be recognized as such. The tremendous social and structural changes in the post-exilic community did, in ways which are difficult for us now to trace in all details, mitigate against the continuance of prophecy. In particular, we can recall that prophecy arose historically at the time when the monarchy began (it was the prophet Samuel who anointed both Saul and David); prophecy flourished during the days of the monarchy when the prophet was often intimately involved with the king, court and international politics. When the kingship ended and Judah was reduced to an insignificant province on the boundaries of the Persian empire, when priesthood and Temple became foundational to the organization of the community, this radical change in the political-social situation must have had a real effect on the continuance of prophecy.

(3) Finally, there is a relationship, again difficult to trace in all the details, between the end of prophecy and the establishment

of a fixed and set body of sacred texts seen as normative for the community—that is, a Canon. As Blenkinsopp observes in a helpful study which develops this point further, "The eclipse of prophecy as an observable reality and the canonization of prophetic writings are related events which cannot be understood apart." [12] As the community became more focused on a determined written text, it became harder to find a place for the charismatic spirit of prophecy. Revelation was now to be found more through the pondering of an early written text, whether by the sage or the apocalyptic seer, rather than in a new word of the Lord spoken through the prophet.

It was precisely in these centuries in which the living word of prophecy "died," that the words of the earlier prophets were collected, edited and transmitted. If prophecy per se were despised, or if the earlier prophets were judged as passé because their words had been accomplished, or as failures because their words had not been fulfilled, there would have been little impetus for the community to preserve, edit, update, and ponder the words of "the former prophets" (Zech 1:4). The fact that we have a section of the Bible called "the Prophets" is a living testimony to the new way in which the spirit of prophecy lived on within the community.

Although it is true that after a certain time prophecy was not considered a functioning institution, the decision to wait "until there should come a prophet to tell them what to do" (1 Mac 4:46) reflects the belief in an eschatological prophet, the tradition of a prophet yet to come. This prophet is variously described in terms of Elijah (Mal 4:5) or Moses (Deut 18:15). Though prophecy might not be a living institution now, it

---

[12]J. Blenkinsopp, *Prophecy and Canon*, (University of Notre Dame Press, 1977), p. 99.

would be revived in the last days (for a somewhat different expression of a future outpouring of the prophetic spirit, see the discussion of Joel 2:28, (pp. 155-157). This tradition of a prophet to come is probably most familiar to us as it appears in the Gospels. John the Baptist is claimed as "Elijah who is to come" (Matt 11:14; also Matt 17:10-13, Mk 6:15). Even Jesus is considered by some as "Elijah or Jeremiah or one of the prophets" (Matt 16:14; also Jn 7:40).

Today, in the Church, there is much concern about how institutions develop and change. Often we are disturbed and frightened to see what is happening to certain institutions (whether an institution as major as the particular form of religious life which has evolved over the last centuries, or as minor as Sunday night Benediction). The institutions which once seemed so stable and permanent now seem to be in continual flux or even in the throes of death. But this is not a new phenomenon for God's people, nor even necessarily a portent of disaster. In our study of the history of prophecy, we see how a major institution of the Old Testament changed radically at the time of the Exile, developed new forms which served for a time, and then faded from the pages of history. Our study of biblical prophecy can make us more sensitive to how God might be at work today, paradoxically, in the transformation and even in the death of those very institutions which seem most sacred.

2

THE HISTORICAL SITUATION

Before we turn to examine some of the dominant themes of the post-exilic prophets, it will be helpful to take a few pages and look more systematically at the historical and political situation. This arrangement of the material is not meant to imply an absolute break between history and spirituality. But it does recognize that we need some concrete historical framework into which to fit the various individual prophets and the specific passages which we will be discussing in the rest of this volume. Prophecy never existed as a timeless, free-floating entity; the prophets spoke within specific historical circumstances; if we are to understand their words we must at least begin with some sense of that framework.

Within the confines of this volume, we can only skim lightly over a general history of the period from 600-300 BC, offering a brief summary of the content of each of the major prophetic books. Any of the standard history books of the Old Testament can be consulted for more extensive treatment.[1] Of

---

[1] In addition to regular histories of the Old Testament, I would recommend the following for more extensive treatment of our period and topic: Joseph Blenkinsopp, *A History of Prophecy in Israel*, (Westminster Press, 1983); Peter Ackroyd, *Exile and Restoration: A Study of Hebrew Thought of the Sixth Century BC*,

course, let us not neglect the bible itself as a fundamental resource; as someone has remarked, "Read the Bible—it does illuminate the commentaries!" Within the Scriptures, in addition to the prophetic books which we will be examining, 2 Kings 22-25 covers the history from the reign of Josiah (640 BC) to the time of the Exile itself (ending with the release of King Jehoiachim from prison in 560 BC). Ezra 1-6 deals with the events of the return and the rebuilding of the Temple (although as a historical source the book of Ezra must be used with caution); Ezra 7-10 and the book of Nehemiah are our main sources of information for the fifth century BC.

A Note On Terminology: Jews, Judaism

Before proceeding, let me say a word about terminology. As we move into the period after 586 BC, more and more we will see and use the terms "Jews" and "Judaism." Prior to 586, the term *yehudim* (Jews) referred only to members of the tribe of Judah, or to citizens of the southern kingdom of Judah (as opposed to the kingdom of Israel in the north). After 586, the term came to be used, not of a political and geographical entity, but of all who stood in the heritage of the pre-exilic Kingdom and followed the religion of YHWH, whether they lived in Palestine, Babylon, Egypt or elsewhere. Thus, all those called Jews shared a common religiocultural heritage, but could, and did, live widely scattered throughout the known world (the Diaspora).

(SCM Press, 1968); Ralph Klein, *Israel in Exile: A Theological Interpretation*, (Fortress, 1979); Walter Brueggemann, *Hopeful Imagination: Prophetic Voices in Exile*, (Fortress, 1986).

Scholars often use the terminology the "Israelite religion" when describing the pre-exilic period; in describing the post-exilic period, particularly after the consolidation and focus on the Law introduced by the scribe Ezra, they talk of "Judaism." More specifically, the Second Temple Period (that is, the years when the Second Temple was in existence, 515 BC—70 AD) is called "Early Judaism." This term "Early Judaism" marks a significant change from last century when, particularly in German scholarship, it was customary to use the terminology "Late Judaism" (Spätjudentum) for the same period, a designation which effectively denied the fact that 2,000 years later Judaism is still very much a living religion.

The Exile As History

In 612 BC, after some three hundred years of unprecedented power and unprecedented cruelty, the mighty Assyrian Empire collapsed. That seemingly invincible conqueror, the kingdom of "unceasing evil" (Nah 3:19) whom so many weaker neighbors had feared for so long was defeated by a combination of external pressure and internal weakness. The main external enemy was the rising power of the Babylonians, another Semitic people centered at the ancient city of Babylon. After a short-lived struggle with Egypt and a clear victory at the battle of Carchemish (605 BC), Babylon established itself as the undisputed power in the Near East.

Although the northern kingdom of Israel had disappeared after being conquered by the Assyrians in 722 BC, the small kingdom of Judah in the south had managed to survive by paying tribute and pledging subservience, first to Assyria and then to Babylon. But in 601 BC king Jehoiachim withdrew allegiance and refused to pay tribute. The Babylonian army under king Nebuchadnezzar quickly marched on Jerusalem in 598 BC, just after king Jehoiachim died. After a short siege, the city surrendered on March 16, 597 BC. The temple was stripped of its treasure, and the new boy-king Jehoiachin, along with other members of the royal family, nobles, land-owners, craftsmen, priests and prophets were taken to Babylon as captives (2 Kgs 24:1-20). In a very real sense, this deportation in 597 was the beginning of what has come to be known historically as "the Exile."

The Babylonians placed Zedekiah, an uncle of Jehoiachin, on the throne of Judah as a vassal king; his rule lasted for eleven years. Sometime in the late 590s or early 580s, "Zedekiah rebelled against the king of Babylon" (2 Kgs 24:20) though the exact details and precise reasons are unknown. Nebuchadnezzar marched again into Judah. The surrounding towns fell one by one; Jerusalem was besieged; the temple was destroyed; the walls of the city were torn down; Zedekiah was blinded and carried off in fetters to Babylon, never to be heard of again (2 Kgs 24:20-25:26). The Babylonians then appointed Gedaliah, a non-Davidite (2 Kgs 25:22); his precise legal status is unclear (governor?, king?), but he was soon assassinated, an event which may have precipitated the final deportation in 581 BC (Jer 52:30).

The Prophets Jeremiah And Ezekiel

The lifetime of the prophet Jeremiah spanned these crucial years. Called by God in 627 BC, he was actively involved in the critical political and religious events of the next forty years; the last we hear of him is around the year 582 BC when he was

deported with his compatriots to Egypt (Jer 43). The book of
Jeremiah is an indispensable source for our understanding of
these last days of the monarchy; yet, it must be read with care.
In the form in which it has come down to us, the book is not a
straight "history" as we understand the term today, nor is it
either an autobiography or a biography of the prophet; rather,
it is a complex collection of different types of material. It
includes actual poetic oracles of Jeremiah (especially in chapters
1-25) and biographical accounts about the prophet, perhaps
written by his scribe Baruch (chs 26-45). These are combined
with many sections written in prose (for example chapters 7,
16, 21) which contain homily-like material, very similar in
language and theology to the book of Deuteronomy. All of this
material has been selected, compiled and reinterpreted by an
editor, who shaped and probably supplemented the material
so that God's word would continue to speak to the generation
after the Exile, and so that Jeremiah could serve as the model
and paradigm of the prophet, par excellence.

Jeremiah was acutely aware of the people's continued
rebellion against a loving God who had entered into covenant
relationship with them. Like Hosea before him, Jeremiah did
not hesitate to speak of their infidelity in the vivid language of
harlotry: "Surely as a faithless wife deserts her husband, so
you have been faithless to me, O house of Israel" (Jer 3:20, also
2:2-3, 3:12-20). Even the Temple in Jerusalem, the site of
divine presence, was no guarantee of divine protection. In a
powerful "temple sermon" (Jer 7 and 26), the prophet mocks
the false confidence and self-delusion of those who act as if it
were enough to say "this is the temple of the Lord, the temple
of the Lord, the temple of the Lord" (Jer 7:4); God could and
would destroy even that sacred institution just as the sanctuary
of Shiloh had been destroyed in days past. Jeremiah might beg,

intercede and warn the people, but in the face of their continued intransigence, he must announce the Lord's verdict of doom, both in words "for I bring evil from the north and great destruction" (Jer 4:6), and in deed, by not taking a wife nor having children, for "behold I will make to cease from this place . . . the voice of mirth and the voice of gladness, the voice of the bridegroom and the voice of the bride" (Jer 16:9). The world as known must come to an end.

But even Jeremiah was called not only "to pluck up and to break down, to destroy and to overthrow (1:10). In at least a limited way, he was to offer the faint outline of a vision of hope; his prophetic task was also "to build and to plant" (Jer 1:10). In the midst of the final battle, with the enemy at the gates and the city poised to fall, Jeremiah went out to buy the ancestral field in his hometown (chapter 32), a concrete pledge that normality would one day return and "houses and fields and vineyards shall again be bought in this land" (Jer 32:15). To the exiles in Babylon, those who might seem to be in the direst straits, he writes of the Lord's plans, "plans for welfare and not for evil, to give you a future and a hope" (Jer 29:11).

While Jeremiah was God's messenger to the people in Judah, the prophet Ezekiel spoke to those exiled in Babylon, so that "they will know that there has been a prophet among them" (Ezek 2:5). A member of a priestly family in Jerusalem, Ezekiel was probably among the deportees sent to Babylon in 597 BC. He received his prophetic call in Babylon in 593 BC and remained active until 571 BC. The book of Ezekiel, as we know it today, is also the product of considerable editorial activity, as seen in the ordering and in the addition of much secondary "priestly" material designed to make the words of the prophet durable and significant for subsequent generations.

Ezekiel is a difficult book. As one scholar describes it, "Amos is perhaps the most inexorable of the critical prophets; Isaiah the most mighty eloquent, and Jeremiah the most sensitive; but Ezekiel is the strangest of them all."[2] Already in the first century AD, Rabbi Hananiah ben Hezekiah is said to have burned three hundred jars of oil in his night vigils as he attempted to explain and defend the book!

Ezekiel receives his call as a prophet in the Temple in an awesome and scarcely describable vision (chapters 1-3) of the chariot throne of God and "the appearance of the likeness of the glory of the Lord" (Ezek 1:29). His call culminates with the commission "I have made you a watchman for the house of Israel" (Ezek 3:16); he will pronounce judgement on both the house of Israel (chapters 4-24) and the foreign nations (25-32). Distinct to Ezekiel is the profound sense of the majesty and absolute otherness of God; God acts with absolute freedom so that "you will know that I am the Lord" (a favorite formula repeated over eighty times). Above all, God is free even to leave the Temple, the place of pollution and apostasy; Ezekiel sees the cloud of God's glory rising up from the Temple and moving off to the east (Ezek 8:1-11:23). But, when the fall of the city of Jerusalem is announced in Babylon, Ezekiel looks not to past sinfulness but to future hope. In what is probably his best known vision (Ezek 37), that of "dem bones, dem dry bones," Ezekiel describes the restoration of the people: "I will put my Spirit within you, and you shall live, and I will place you in your own land (Ezek 37:14). In the final chapters (40-48), Ezekiel the priest outlines a detailed plan for the restoration of the Temple, in anticipation of that

[2]Klaus Koch, *The Prophets: The Babylonian and Persian Period*, (Fortress, 1978, 1984), p. 86.

day when once again the glory of the Lord will fill the Temple and "the name of the city henceforth shall be 'The Lord is there'" (Ezek 48:35).

The Exile As Crisis

It is more difficult than it seems at first glance to give a realistic assessment of the Exile. One picture can be drawn from the Book of Lamentations, a series of five haunting poems which lament the destruction of Jerusalem. The city is described as desolate:

> How lonely sits the city that was full of people!
> How like a widow has she become,
> she that was great among the nations! (Lam 1:1)

> Mount Zion lies desolate;
> jackals prowl over it (Lam 5:18);

her Temple profaned:

> She has seen the nations invade her sanctuary,
> those whom you did forbid to enter your congregation"
> (Lam 1:10);

her people are slain:

> In the dust of the streets lie the young and the old;
> my maidens and my young men have fallen by the sword;
> in the day of your anger you have slain them,
> slaughtering without mercy (Lam 2:21);

or facing starvation:

> The hands of compassionate women have boiled their own
> children;

they became their food in the destruction . . . (Lam 4:10).

In one poignant passage (which is perhaps more familiar to generations of Catholics from its adaptation in the Reproaches of the Good Friday liturgy), the city Zion speaks:

> Is it nothing to you, all you who pass by?
> Look and see
> if there is any sorrow like my sorrow
> which was brought upon me,
> which the Lord inflicted
> on the day of his fierce anger (Lam 1:12).

The author of Chronicles paints a similar picture of near-total destruction; drawing upon a different metaphor, he describes how "the land lay desolate" to keep a sabbath for seventy years (2 Chr 36:21).

Yet such texts cannot be taken as the definitive historical description of the exilic condition; each has a purpose beyond the mere recounting of historical "fact." Chronicles is giving a theological interpretation in the language of sabbath rest. Lamentations is drawing upon sterotypical language (which was by the time of the Exile already over a thousand years old) for the description of a conquered city; we can find many of the exact same descriptive phrases in the Sumerian poem "Lament Over the Destruction of Ur" written in 2000 BC. Against the descriptions of a land bereft of its population must be placed texts such as 2 Kgs 24:14, 16 and Jer 52:28-30 which give figures of a total of five to ten thousand people deported. On the one hand, the expulsion of the religious, intellectual and political leaders would have seriously disrupted the social fabric of Judah and created a vacuum in land ownership and political leadership; but, on the other hand, probably only a small percentage of the total population was actually uprooted.

The Babylonians did not practice mass explusion as did the Assyrians, nor total genocide of conquered peoples such as we, unfortunately, have known in our modern times. Similarly, although there was certainly heavy destruction of crops and the attendant spectre of starvation, in the fall of the year after the destruction of Jerusalem the people who were left in the land "gathered wine and summer fruits in great abundance" (Jer 40:12).

The conditions of the exiles in Babylon call for similar critical investigation. Certainly there is no evidence that they were kept in concentration-like camps or subjected to harsh labor. Early in the Exile, Jeremiah wrote to those in Babylon to "Build houses and live in them; plant gardens and eat their produce. Take wives and have sons and daughters . . ." (Jer 29:5-6), an exhortation which assumes that all of this was at least possible. A number of passages in Ezekiel ("then came certain elders of Israel and sat before me" Ezek 14:1, 20:1, 33:30) suggest freedom of assembly and preservation of community structure, although this may just be a standardized literary convention for introducing a sermon. It is clear that when Cyrus did allow the Jews to return to Palestine, there was no overwhelming rush to leave Babylon. Many Jews had learned that it was indeed possible to sing the songs of the Lord in a foreign land; they chose to stay permanently and formed the beginning of what was to be a significant Diaspora community which prospered on into the Middle Ages.

Although physical conditions, both for those left in the land and for those in exile, may not have been as harsh as we sometimes envision, Judah was still a conquered nation. It had lost it independence as a political entity, its king, and its Temple. The seeds of future socio-economic and theological conflict were sown. On the one hand, there were those who had remained in the land and thus claimed that God was on their side, "They have gone far from the Lord; to us this land is surely given as a possession" (Ezek 11:15; see also 33:23); others claimed that God was definitely with those who passed through the experience of exile, "Like these good figs, so I will regard as good the exiles from Judah, whom I have sent away from this place to the land of the Chaldeans" (Jer 24:5).

A twentieth century political scientist could read the events of 587 BC in a purely secular way—that is, a small vassal state which had somehow managed to survive the previous - tumultuous century as a minor but independent actor on the stage of world history, finally succumbed to the inevitable and was swallowed up by the expansionist Babylonian Empire. But, for the biblical writers, the events had a theological meaning and provoked a four-fold crisis of faith; they called into question the very foundations of Judah's traditional belief about the king, the land, the Temple and the nature of her God:

(1) The succession of kings in Judah, right down to the days of Zedekiah, was seen as a living fulfillment of the eternal promise made to David: "Your house and your kingdom shall be made sure for ever before me; your throne shall be established for ever" (2 Sam 7:16). But what happened to this divine promise when "the breath of our nostrils, the Lord's anointed was taken in their pits" (Lam 4:20) and the Davidic monarchy seemed at an end?

(2) The possession of the land was the fulfillment of the promise to Abraham "To your descendants I will give this land" (Gen 12:7). Was this promise null and void now that the land, Israel's inheritance, was in the hands of foreigners?

(3) The Temple was the visible sign of God's presence, "the place of which you have said, 'My name shall be there'" (1 Kgs

8:29). The sacred mountain, Mount Zion, was the link between heaven and earth, the very "navel of the world" (Ezek
5:5, 38:12). How was communication possible between the
divine and human when the Temple lay in ruins, and the
sacrifices could no longer be offered?

(4) What about the power and fidelity of YHWH? While it
may be true that there are no atheists in foxholes, there was no
guarantee that the experience of calamity would automatically
lead to a return to the true God. Jeremiah described how some
of the people gave their own interpretation of the reasons for
the disaster which had befallen them:

> As for the word which you have spoken to us in the name of the
> Lord, we will not listen to you. But we will do everything that
> we have vowed, burn incense to the queen of heaven, and pour
> out libations to her, as we did, both we and our fathers . . . for
> then we had plenty of food and prospered, and saw no evil. But
> since we left off burning incense to the queen of heaven and
> pouring out libations to her, we have lacked everything and
> have been consumed by the sword and by famine
>
> (Jer 44:16-18).

Certainly the Exile could be interpreted as proving that the
Queen of Heaven (a Canaanite mother goddess) or perhaps
Marduk (the principal god of the Babylonians) was simply
more powerful than YHWH, the God of Judah. Had the Lord
simply abandoned the people, turning away permanently in
disgust? Some of the exiles actually dared to voice the unthink-
able, "The Lord does not see us; the Lord has forsaken the
land" (Ezek 8:12).

The Prophetic Response: Second Isaiah

It was the prophets, above all, who were called to respond to the crisis. Their task was twofold: to force the people to confront the reality of their losses—land, Temple, king—and, even more difficult, to begin the task of reconstruction, of envisioning a new world of the future. We have already seen how, in the days subsequent to the fall of Jerusalem, Jeremiah and Ezekiel began to redefine the task of prophecy. Now was not the time for words of judgement; the judgement was past and God was neither impotent nor finished with his people. The book of Jeremiah uses the bold language of *new* covenant, "I will make a new covenant with the house of Israel and the house of Judah" (Jer 31:31); the book of Ezekiel looks to a new self-declaration of how God is to be known, "I will put my Spirit within you, and you shall live, and I will place you in your own land; then you shall know that I, the Lord, have spoken and I have done it" (Ezek 37:14).

In the days of deepest despair, a prophet living in exile in Babylon was called to speak powerful and poetic words of consolation, "Comfort, comfort my people" (Isa 40:1). Since his oracles come to us today as chapters 40-55 of the book of Isaiah, we call this unnamed individual Second Isaiah or Deutero-Isaiah. (Here I am following the consensus of critical scholarship since the last century which recognizes that the historical situation behind these chapters, their style and vocabulary, and the themes which they develop, all point to the sixth century as the time of their origin, not to the eighth century world of the prophet Isaiah of chapters 1-39. When speaking of this prophet the convention is to say "he," but we don't really even know if this was a man or a woman).

The core of the message is contained in the opening words:

> Comfort, comfort my people,
> says your God.
> speak tenderly to Jerusalem,
> and cry to her,
> that her warfare is ended,
> and her iniquity is pardoned,
> that she has received from the Lord's hand
> double for all her sins"
>
> (Isa 40:1-2)

The time of judgement is over; there is to be a future in which the Lord will act in a new and wonderous way, "Behold, I am doing a new thing; now it springs forth, do you not perceive it?" (Isa 43:19). Rather than the Lord being impotent, it is the gods of Babylon who are exposed and mocked as mere idols (Isa 41:21-29, 46:1-2). In years past, God had spoken, especially through the prophets, "declaring the end from the beginning and from ancient times things not yet done" (Isa 46:10); now, this divine word is still the controlling force behind history, for "the word of our God will stand for ever" (Isa 40:8, also 55:10-11). The God who had been active in the very formation of the cosmos, who "created the heavens and stretched them out, who spread forth the earth and what comes from it" (Isa 42:5), continues to rule history, "drafting" even the seemingly mighty Persian king Cyrus to serve the divine purpose. A correct reading of the current situation indicates that it is YHWH who "says of Cyrus 'He is my shepherd' and he shall fulfill all my purpose" (Isa 44:28). In the end, the only response is that of praise as the prophet bursts forth in song:

> Sing, O heavens, for the Lord has done it
> shout, O depths of the earth . . .

For the Lord has redeemed Jacob,
and will be glorified in Israel

(Isa 44:23).

The Restoration

The Babylonian Empire which had risen so quickly to such mighty power proved to be short-lived. Its final king, - Nabonidus (555-539 BC) was a weak, ineffectual ruler and an eccentric figure, more interested in antiquarian research and the promotion of his favorite cult of the moon god Sin than in the duties of kingship; as the ancient chronicles lament, "The king did not come to Babylon . . . the festival of the New Year was omitted."

Meanwhile, another power was on the rise, the kingdom of the Medes and the Persians. For the first time in some fifteen hundred years, the new rulers of the entire Near East from India to the Aegean, were to be an Indo-European (Aryan) rather than a Semitic people. Their origins and center of power lay in the steppe region to the northeast of the Fertile Crescent. Their leader Cyrus (the Cyrus whom Second Isaiah hailed) quickly took control over the Median kingdom of his father-in-law Astyages and then moved to extend Persian dominance over the whole of Asia Minor and east to modern Pakistan and Afghanistan. In October 539 BC, Cyrus literally walked into Babylon; the Persian chronicles relate how he "entered Babylon as a friend" and with the complicity of the Babylonian officials and the priests of Marduk, he "took the hand of the god Marduk" and was proclaimed king.

As part of his strategy to stabilize and control his empire, Cyrus introduced a general policy of returning captive peoples to their homes and restoring their religious cults. Thus, in 538 BC, he issued an edict (a copy of which is preserved in Ezra 6:1-5) allowing the Jews to return to Jerusalem, authorizing the rebuilding of the Temple with funds from the royal treasury, and ordering the restoration of the temple vessels which had been carried off to Babylon. The Exile per se was over!

In point of fact, it appears that immediately after Cyrus's edict, only a small group of Jews returned under Sheshbazzar, "a prince of Judah" (Ezra 1:8), who was perhaps from the Davidite line. We really know very little about the precise details of the twenty years immediately following, or about the exact administrative arrangements determined by Persia for the governance of the area. Sheshbazzar himself quickly disappeared from the scene. These seem to have been years of poverty, drought and crop failure. Perhaps the foundations of the Temple were laid at this time (see Ezra 5:16), but little more was accomplished. There are traces of bitter conflict and rivalry between those who had remained behind, "the people of the land," and those who were returnees from Babylon, "the sons of the exiles," as well as conflict with the Samaritans (the inhabitants of the area around Samaria to the north).

In 522 BC the whole Persian Empire was shaken by the death of Cambyses. Various claimants and pretenders came forward for the throne and widespread revolts spread throughout the empire as conquered peoples quickly took advantage of the internal weakness of their conquerors. By 520 BC, the crisis was over and Darius was firmly ensconced as king. It was probably during the tumult of these years that another large group of Jews made the trek from Babylon to Jerusalem (Ezra 2:1-70) under the leadership of Zerubbabel, the civil head of the mission (and perhaps a member of the Davidic line), and

Joshua, the high priest. With strong support from the prophets Haggai and Zechariah (whom we will be discussing in a moment), work began in earnest on the rebuilding of the Temple. In March/April 515 BC, the Temple was completed and dedicated, the "Second Temple" destined to stand until the final destruction by the Romans in 70 AD.

The Prophets Haggai and Zechariah

Of all the post-exilic prophets, Haggai and Zechariah are the only two whose oracles come down to us with precise dates given by an editor. Haggai's oracles are dated between August and December 520 BC; Zechariah spoke over a two year period from November 520 to December 518 BC. Thus, we are invited to read their words (at least on one level) in particular relationship to concrete historical events.

Haggai is one of the shortest prophetic books, just some thirty-eight verses in all. For Haggai, the rebuilding of the Temple was an absolute priority. Following the thrust of the priestly tradition, he viewed the Temple as the focus of the restored community, the place where the Lord would appear in glory (Hag 1:8) and the source and guarantee of fertility and prosperity (Hag 2:18-19). In this sense at least, we can talk of Haggai as a "cult prophet"; that is, with Haggai concerns about cult, even the ritual laws of holy/unholy (2:10-19), are part and parcel of the prophetic mandate. Although the rebuilding of the temple with Persian support and money and the pragmatic priestly mentality could make for a very "establishment" outlook, Haggai maintained a lively sense of God's action still to come. The fulfillment was not complete; God would still "shake the heavens and the earth and the sea and the dry land" (Hag 2:6). At a time of political upheaval throughout the empire, this hope for further divine intervention was linked to nationalistic fervor in the person of Zerubbabal, whom Haggai boldly called by such royal terms as "my servant" and "signet ring" (2:23; compare Jer 22:24).

The prophet Zechariah has left us a series of eight "visions in the night" (Zech 1:7—6:15), plus a number of oracles (Zech 1:2-6, 7-8) and some oracular material now interwoven right into the visions (e.g. Zech 4:9-10). Chapters 9-14 of our present book of Zechariah are an anonymous collection from a much later period (see pp. 59-60). In Zechariah's visions, we encounter a strange world—monstrous flying scrolls, a woman in a bushel basket, four horns, a man with a measuring line, four chariots with horses of differing colors—no wonder an interpreter (a *mal'ak* or messenger) is needed to explain what is happening! In form, prophecy is now on the road to the full-blown apocalyptic style we know from Daniel with its even lengthier and more developed visions. By means of this highly symbolic language, Zechariah is boldly presenting a restoration program for the new community, a community purified from evil (chapter 5), in which the Lord will once again dwell "I will be the glory within her" (Zech 2:5). In the figure of the menorah flanked by two olive trees (ch 4), he portrays a new form of leadership by "the two anointed," Joshua the high priest, and Zerubbabel who is given the messianic title "the Branch" (Zech 3:8, 6:12, compare Jer 33:14-16).

The Persian And Hellenistic Period

After these two prophets and the events which surrounded

the building of the Temple, we know almost nothing about the next two hundred years in Judah. Although Haggai and Zechariah had spoken in such blatantly messianic terms, Zerubbabel simply disappeared from the scene and the leadership of the community passed into the hands of the priests. There were certainly prophets at this time (as we will see in a moment), but their prophecies are not dated, nor are they tied to recognizable historical events. Recent archaeological work has shed some light on these "Dark Ages"; from the newly discovered papyri texts from Wadi Daliyeh we can at least suggest the names of the governors and high priests between 515-332 BC, but that is about all. It is one of the ironies of history that we know more about the distant past, the age of King David for instance in the tenth century BC, than we do about the fifth-third centuries BC in Judah.

The curtain lifts briefly in the mid-fifth century to reveal two figures, one a civil governor and the other a scribe. In 445 BC, Nehemiah, a Jewish official in the Persian court, was sent out to Judah as governor, with permission to rebuild the walls of the city which still lay in ruin and disrepair. Nehemiah initiated social and economic reforms, including enforcement of the Sabbath observance, reform of the debt laws, and the prohibition of marriage with foreign wives. About the same time, Ezra, a priest and a scribe "skilled in the law of Moses," (Ezra 7:6) came out from Babylon to Jerusalem to initiate a major religious reform. The exact date of Ezra's visit, whether he predated and overlapped with Nehemiah (arriving in 458 BC), or whether he came after him (arriving in 428 BC or even 398 BC), is one of the famous insoluble questions of biblical history—fortunately it is not our prime concern here! Ezra is described as coming from Babylon "with the law of God in his hand" (Ezra 7:14) which he read to the whole people in a solemn assembly (Neh 8-9), concluding with a renewal of covenant. This law, which was close to (although not identical with) our Pentateuch, became the legal charter for the community, bringing together the traditions and laws of the past as the normative guide for the future. For his establishment of the community on the foundations of Torah and election, Ezra is honored in Jewish tradition with the titles of "the Second Moses," "the father of Judaism."

After Ezra, the curtain descends again. Even the transition from Persian to Greek (Hellenistic) rule left little mark in our biblical books and probably, at least in its intitial stages, in the ordinary life of the people. We know from non-biblical sources that Alexander the Great gained control in Syro-Palestine in 332 BC, as one small stage of his expansive sweep to the East as far as India. After Alexander's premature death in 323 BC, the empire was divided up among his generals, and Palestine passed into the control of the Ptolemies for over a hundred years. The curtain really only begins to rise again after the Seleucids gained control of the area in 198 BC, precipitating the chain of events which led to the Maccabean revolt (167 BC). By that time, as already noted, we have reached the days when prophecy was no longer considered a living reality, when people could only wait "until there should come a prophet to tell them what to do" (1 Macc 4:46).

In the years following Haggai and Zechariah there were a number of prophets in Judah—Third Isaiah, Joel, Malachi, Deutero-Zechariah, the anonymous author of Isaiah 24-27. Since their words come to us undated and cannot be linked to a historical context, many passages seem to be "hanging in the air," or are just plainly obscure or unintelligible. Although this material is difficult and sometimes frustrating and often we come away feeling that we have simply not grasped its point or importance, yet the sheer bulk of texts indicates that prophecy was still living and flourishing during these days.

Third Isaiah

The last chapters of our present book of Isaiah, chapters 56-66, represent the work of one of these unnamed prophets, or perhaps this is a collection of oracles from a number of different prophets—for the sake of simplicity, we will call this whole collection Third (Tritero) Isaiah. Although certain themes and vocabulary remind us of Second Isaiah (and even First Isaiah), the context is clearly different. It is evident that the people are back in their land (i.e., after 538 BC), although it is difficult to know if all or any of the material dates from after the rebuilding of the Temple (515 BC). If Second Isaiah portrayed a magnificent vision of a glorious return, a Way back in glory through a flowering desert, Third Isaiah confronts the harsh reality of conditions after the Restoration and seeks to explain why salvation has not yet come. These chapters reflect sharp, often bitter, inter-community polemic and conflict, apparently centered around the cult and priesthood; these prophecies clearly come from the losing group, those who feel they have been marginalized, cut off from their true role in the community. Furthermore, in contrast to the earlier prophets who spoke to the entire people, now in this split community there is a word of judgement for some, a word of salvation for others: "Behold *my servants* shall eat, but *you* shall be hungry . . . *my servants* shall rejoice, but *you* shall be put to shame" (65:13). Throughout, the prophet maintains a lively sense that God will again intervene in a wondrous way; hope lies not in the present, but in the eschatological expectation that "soon my salvation will come, and my deliverance will be revealed" (56:1). What is now is not the fulfillment of the promises; there are still to come "new heavens and a new earth" (65:17).

Joel

This short work of some three chapters (or four, if your translation of the Bible is following the Hebrew division of the verses) is a puzzling book. It opens with a vivid description of the horror of a locust plague wreaking havoc in the land. Scholars still debate whether parts of these chapters may be pre-exilic and whether the locust attacks refer to an actual catastrophe or are an allegory for the onslaught of the foreign nations. The first two chapters contain the main elements of a penitential liturgy: "Rend your hearts and not your garments. Return to the Lord your God, for he is gracious and merciful, slow to anger, and abounding in steadfast love and repents of evil" (Joel 2:13). The last segment of the book looks to the future when God will come as a warrior on the day of the final battle; on this Day of the Lord all nations will be gathered in the Valley of Jehoshaphat for the final act of judgement. But, for Israel, on that day, the spirit will be poured out so that "your sons and daughters shall prophesy" (Joel 2:28).

Malachi

From the book of Malachi itself, we know neither the exact date nor even the name of the prophet; the title simply comes from the opening words of chapter 3 which in the Hebrew reads *malachi* "my messenger." Even a cursory reading of the first two chapters indicates that the prophet was active after the rebuilding of the Temple, but probably before the reforms of Ezra and Nehemiah; certain linguistic features of the language also point to the early fifth century. The book consists of six oracles in the specific form of a disputation, that is, a rhetorical question addressed to God or the people, and an answer by the prophet in God's name. Malachi is concerned with specific manifestations of the collapse of religious enthusiasm: the offering of sick animals for sacrifice, priestly neglect of cultic duties, marriage with non-Jewish women, social inequality in the community. The Temple has been rebuilt, but the eschatological age has not yet come, the Day of the Lord which will bring judgement to the wicked and salvation to the just. The very last verses (Mal 4:4-6, or 3:22-24 in the Hebrew numbering of the verses) are added as a colophon to the whole prophetic corpus, announcing the coming of the prophet Elijah "before the great and terrible day of the Lord" (4:5).

Zechariah 9-14

These final chapters of our present book of Zechariah are difficult both to understand and to date. Sometimes scholars even divide them further into Deutero-Zechariah (9-11) and Tritero-Zechariah (12-14). Specific phrases from these prophecies are quite familiar to us, owing to the fact that they were taken up by the Gospel writers in the description of Jesus's passion: e.g., "your king comes to you . . . humble and riding on an ass" (9:9), "they weighed out as my wages thirty shekels of silver" (11:12), "when they look on him whom they have pierced" (12:10).

For linguistic and stylistic reasons, we should perhaps date these chapters rather early, that is fifth century BC (about the same time as Malachi), though in the past scholars have tended to put them much later (in the fourth or even third century BC). Permeating the whole book is a strong eschatological sense of the Day of the Lord which is to come, the day of the final battle, when the whole world is to be judged, "and the Lord will become king over all the earth" (14:9).

Isaiah 24-27

These three chapters, presently found in the midst of First Isaiah, really belong with late prophecy. Although not an apocalpyse in the strict sense of the term (as the book of Daniel is), they are often called the "Isaiah Apocalypse." Again the dating is very uncertain; suggestions range from 500 BC down to 200 BC. Although much of the material is so obscure that there is no agreement even as to what city is being described (25:1-5, 26:1-6), other passages clearly describe the eschatological banquet on Mount Zion and the final victory of God, even over the power of death itself (Isa 25:6-8).

In a matter of twenty pages or so, we have been able to do no more than trace the flow of history between 600—300 BC and to indicate something of the who and the what of the various prophets in this period. Whenever a picture is painted with such broad strokes, there is much left out, much that needs more careful nuancing. But I am convinced that such a general orientation is essential before we turn to the specific passages from these prophets which we will be examining in the rest of this book. If you have been somewhat overwhelmed either by the amount of material covered or the superficiality of the treatment, or even simply bored by "so much history," be assured that we are now ready to focus on specific biblical texts.

3

"IN BORROWED IMAGES"

There are many different places where we could begin in our attempt to articulate the spirituality of the post-exilic prophets. Let us start with the most basic—an examination of what these prophets have to say about God.

In much recent theological writing, there has been renewed reflection on the nature of "God-language." Some fifteen hundred years ago, St. Augustine recognized that when we, as human beings, attempt to talk about God we are immediately caught up in an inextricable bind. While it may be possible for an individual to communicate *with* God in the innermost depths of one's being "with sighs too deep for words" (Rom 8:26), when, as a community, we want to talk either *to* God or *about* God, we necessarily require human language. And yet, the Divine, by definition, cannot be encompassed in mere human words. To paraphrase Augustine, if we describe the Infinite in finite human language, what we have described is not the Infinite!

Recently, Patrick D. Miller, Professor of Old Testament Theology at Princeton Theological Seminary, attempted to outline a series of simple, basic theses which are foundational to any discussion of God-language.[1] His first two theses express a fundamental paradox:

1. God Is God And Not A Human Being

Obvious as this thesis may be, it is the foundation of everything else that must be said. God is above, beyond, apart from all sexual distinctions and human categories. All personalistic and anthropomorphic language about God, while real, is also symbolic, indirect, analogical and partial.

2. God Is, Nevertheless, To Be Conceived Of And Is Known in Personal Categories

There is an obvious and appropriate tension between this thesis and the preceding one. The tension must be maintained, however, because the first thesis means that we are always speaking analogically about God when we use human language, while the revelation of God in Jesus Christ means that the analogical language participates in and reflects the reality to which it points but is not identical with it and does not exhaust it.

The language of the bible knows this paradox when it comes to speaking about God. In fact, this is part of what we mean when, to use a traditional formulation, we talk of Sacred Scripture as "the Word of God in human words." The Constitution on Divine Revelation of the Second Vatican Council (paragraph 13), in describing how "the words of God, expressed in human language, have been made like human discourse," takes up the words of St. John Chrysostom to recall the marvelous "condescension" by which "we may learn the gentle kindness of God, which words cannot express, and

[1]Patrick D. Miller, "Theses on the Gender of God," *Haelen: A Journal on the State of the Art of Worship, Prayer and Meditation Practice* 6, 1985, pp. 4-8.

how far he has gone in adapting His language with thoughtful concern for our weak human nature." Or, to quote St. Ephrem of Syria, God is always revealed to us "clothed in borrowed images."

So it is that when the prophets attempted to talk of God, they chose the language of metaphor (God is a shepherd) or the language of analogy (God is good). In order to speak about the unspeakable, they described God in comparison with something else which originated in their experience of created reality; as St. Thomas Aquinas recognized, "Holy Scripture delivers spiritual things to us beneath metaphors taken from bodily things." The prophets used a plethora of images, metaphors, similes and titles, some of which are very familiar to us (God as father, king, potter, judge, husband, shepherd, rock), others of which are less well known (God as mother—see pp. 79-82; eagle—Deut 32:11; dew—Hos 14:5; lion—Hos 5:14, 13:7; she-bear—Hos 13:8). This very multiplicity of images is important as it, in itself, reminds us that God can neither be contained in one image nor encompassed by all taken together. Such rich metaphorical language helps us to avoid the most pervasive of all temptations—that of idolatry, the temptation to take as God something which is not God. The idol which the law of Deuteronomy warns about can be "in any form whatsoever" (Deut 4:16), even a name or an image. When we use language metaphorically, our language is "like a finger pointing to the moon. To equate the finger with the moon or to acknowledge the finger and not perceive the moon is to miss the point."[2]

Having accepted the inevitability of using metaphorical language in our God-talk, it is most instructive to look

[2]Phyllis Trible, *God and the Rhetoric of Sexuality*, (Fortress Press, 1978), p. 16.

specifically and consciously at *what* particular metaphors are used by the prophets to tease the mind into creative reflection. In the following pages, I have chosen to explore four ways of talking about God which are to be found (in addition to other traditional images) in the post-exilic prophets: God as redeemer, God as father, God as mother, God as warrior.

God As Redeemer

We will begin by examining a number of passages in which God is called redeemer. The language of redeemer/redemption is certainly part of our Christian religious vocabulary; to confirm this, we need only recall some of our hymns (powerful fashioners of the imagination) such as "To Jesus Christ, our Sovereign King" with its climactic conclusion "Christ Jesus, Lord and Redeemer," or the lilting Dutch melody "We praise Thee, O God, our Redeemer, Creator." Although our understanding of the term is shaped by its distinctive Christian usage, (despite the fact that throughout the centuries of Christian thought attempts to formulate a "theology" of redemption have been surprisingly elusive), yet the fact is that the basic concept is solidly rooted in the Old Testament.

It is the prophet Second Isaiah, above all, who brought the term redeemer into central focus. The noun "Redeemer" (*go'el* in Hebrew) occurs some ten times, and the verb "redeem, release" (*ga'al*) an additional seven times, which is an impressive concentration in fifteen relatively short chapters. Third Isaiah, continuing the same theological trajectory, takes up the root a further six times, and Isaiah 35 (which has close affinities to Second Isaiah, if not actually from the same hand) talks likewise of "the redeemed" (Isa 35:9). Clearly Second

Isaiah did not invent the metaphor; it is to be found in a few pre-exilic texts (e.g. Gen 48:16, Ex 15:13, Hos 13:14), and in a few psalms (both pre- and post-exilic).

But why would Second Isaiah choose this metaphor, this particular way to describe God's activity at this time of crisis? By calling God Redeemer (go'el), Second Isaiah is fixing upon a metaphor taken from the realm of family law; in a secular context, the word go'el is normally translated "kinsman." This is a technical term for a specific blood relation within the tribal structure, the next of kin, who is obliged to the duty of redemption (ge'ulla) in specific circumstances when something belonging to the clan has been lost. In particular, the kinsman is called to redeem the life of those who have been obliged to sell themselves into slavery because of penury (Lev 25:47-55); to redeem the life of one murdered by executing the guilty (Num 35:31-34, the "Redeemer of Blood)"; to redeem the life of a husband who died without children by marrying the widow and giving the name and property of the deceased husband to the first son (Deut 25:5-10, and the book of Ruth); to redeem the land which an Israelite is forced to sell before it can be bought by outsiders (Lev 25:23-34). Unlike other verbs of redemption and release which are more general or which come from the realm of commercial law, this term highlights the bond of kinship between redeemer and redeemed.

Thus, to the disillusioned exiles in Babylon in their time of loss, as they lament "The Lord has forsaken me, my Lord has forgotten me" (Isa 49:14), Second Isaiah offers the assurance that God still stands in relationship to them as their go'el. True, they have been "sold" into slavery; now God as their redeemer is obliged to come to their rescue. At a time when the traditional language of covenant was fraught with ambiguity (when some asked whether the covenant(s) of the past were still valid or whether they had been irrevocably broken), the language of Redeemer was able to combine the element of divine obligation with the more personal dimension of kinship relationship. The deliverance promised will not be totally new, not a radical dissonance with the past; rather, it will be the restoration of what has been lost. Thus, the term calls to mind the first mighty act of redemption "I am the Lord, and I will bring you out from under the burdens of the Egyptians, and I will deliver you from their bondage, and will *redeem* you with an outstretched arm and with great acts of judgement" (Ex 6:6).

Recognizing the importance of the term in Second Isaiah, let us look briefly at one specific passage to see how God is described as Redeemer. Here, as in subsequent discussion when we pause to look at a particular text, the intention is not to provide a thorough exposition of everything which can or should be said about the passage; rather, I will pick out a few main points and trust that the reader will refer to a standard commentary for a more complete study.

Isaiah 43:1-7:

> But now thus says the Lord,
> he who created you, O Jacob,
> he who formed you, O Israel:
> "Fear not, for I have redeemed you;
> I have called you by name, you are mine."
>
> (43:1)

This poem introduces us to an Oracle of Salvation, one of the basic units of speech in Second Isaiah. The oracle starts with a typical message formula "thus says the Lord," announcing this as the word of the Lord, not of Marduk or any of the

Babylonian idols. God is identified as "the one who created you, O Jacob; the one who formed you, O Israel"; we will recall in a moment this distinctive usage of the language of creation. Then we hear the command "fear not," followed immediately by the reason "for I have redeemed you." This is not a vague, ethereal admonition for confidence, but is rooted in the certainty that Israel has a *go'el* to come to her rescue. The Revised Standard Version translation "I have redeemed you" is a "prophetic perfect" verb, referring not so much to a past action, but to what is with certainty about to happen; perhaps it would be better translated "I redeem you." As the verse concludes, the deliverance is set even more firmly in personal terms, "I have called you by name, you are mine."

In verses 2-4, the poet continues the imagery of ransoming and freeing from slavery. The redeemed will pass through obstacles. The water may have a particular reference to the waters of the Exodus, or the water and fire may signify any disaster (compare Ps 66:12 "we went through fire and through water; yet you have brought us forth to a spacious place)." Verse 3 contains one of Second Isaiah's strong affirmations "For I am the Lord Your God, the Holy One of Israel, your Saviour." The terminology "the Holy One" comes from First Isaiah (Isa 1:4, chapter 6, etc.); it names the God who is separate and other. Yet, this Holy One is also Redeemer, bound to Israel by the obligations of kinship; in fact, the version of this verse found in the great Isaiah manuscript of Qumran (1QIsa^a) reads here "The Holy One of Israel, your Redeemer," a striking combination of titles which occurs frequently in Second Isaiah (41:14, 43:14, 47:4, 49:7, 54:5). The image of redemption is carried forward into verses 3b and 4; without reducing these lines to a straight literalistic interpretation on the historical plane, the point is made that the

Redeemer is willing to pay a heavy price as a ransom "because you are precious in my eyes, and honored, and I love you" (43:4).

The last lines of this oracle (43:7), taken together with the first, form an "inclusio" which envelops this poem with creation language: "who created you O Jacob, who formed you, O Israel" (verse 1) and "whom I created for my glory, whom I formed and made" (verse 7). God's redeeming action in restoring the exiles to their land is to be seen as a new act of creation. It is one of the distinctive contributions of Second Isaiah's theological creativity to bring the two ideas of redemption and creation together in this new way: the confidence in the power of God to redeem, so contrary to a surface reading of the historical situation, is rooted in God's creative activity in the very fashioning of the cosmos (e.g., Isa 40:26, 42:5, 44:24).

In Conclusion:

In a number of other texts (which we can only mention briefly), Second Isaiah draws in even more aspects of the Redeemer obligation. God is the avenging redeemer of blood, the violent destroyer of the murderer, "I will make your oppressors eat their own flesh, and they shall be drunk with their own blood as with wine. Then all flesh shall know that I am the Lord your Saviour, and your Redeemer, the Mighty One of Jacob" (Isa 49:26; see also 47:3). In a complicated poem in chapter 54:1-17, there is perhaps a hint that God is also the kinsman spouse to Israel who finds herself without husband or children. Third Isaiah later links the language of redemption with the forgiveness of sins, "And he will come to Zion as Redeemer, to those in Jacob who turn from transgression" (Isa 59:20), pointing obliquely to the line of development to be taken up in the New Testament (Col 1:14).

In his own day, when Second Isaiah repeatedly introduced this language of Redeemer, it must have sounded new and strange to his audience. Surely some asked, "Why not just keep with the old ways of talking about God—king, shepherd, Holy One?" But in radically changed circumstances, when the people regarded themselves as having been abandoned into slavery in Babylon, Second Isaiah looked to an unfamiliar image of God, something which resonanted with their experience and yet opened their collective imagination to a new way of understanding the possibilities of how God might act. It is a metaphor which was given a new dimension by the early Christians and which lives on today in our vocabulary, our prayers and hymns, even though we might be hard pressed to explain it rationally or even theologically.

God As Father

As Christians, probably our most familiar image of God is as father. We "have the courage to say" (in the words of the Roman Missal) the prayer which Jesus taught us, "Our Father, who art in heaven . . . ." This is the first prayer which we learned as children, the center of our daily devotions, the prayer which is recited every time the Eucharist is celebrated, and the prayer which will be said when we are laid to rest in the grave. Furthermore, the Gospels portray Jesus addressing God as Father *Abba* (for example, Mk 14:36, in Gethsemane, and Lk 23:46, on the Cross). Because we are children of God through baptism, "God has sent the Spirit of his Son into our hearts, crying, 'Abba! Father!' " (Gal 4:6). It is surprising then to realize how relatively infrequently this particular metaphor occurs in the Old Testament.

The concept of God as father was certainly very ancient, sometimes finding expression in such personal names as Eliab (Num 1:9) which means "God is [my] father." But a survey of the biblical attestations reveals that God is called Father only some twenty times in the whole of the Old Testament. Six of these passages are from the very latest books (Tobit 13:4, Wisdom 2:16, 14:3, Ben Sira 23:1, 23:4, 51:10). In five of the occurrences, the language of father is specifically in terms of the Davidic king and God's adoption of the king at the royal coronation: "I will be his father, and he will be my son" (2 Sam 7:14, 1 Chr 17:13, 22:10, 28:6, Ps 89:26). In addition, there are a number of other places where the image is of God as father even though the specific term is not employed (for example, Deut 8:5, "As a man disciplines his son, the Lord your God disciplines you").

Of the texts in which God is actually called father, seven come from the prophets Jeremiah, Third Isaiah and Malachi. This language seems to have been avoided by the pre-exilic prophets, perhaps because of the danger that the fatherhood of God would be interpreted in a physical or mythological sense, as in the neighboring pagan religions. Thus, it is only these three exilic and post-exilic prophets who dare to say of God "You are our father" (Isa 64:8).

Let us look now more closely at these seven texts in order to determine what it meant for the prophets to call God father.

Malachi 1:6:

> A son honors his father, and a servant his master. If then I am a father, where is my honor? And if I am a master, where is my fear?

These questions introduce a long passage (1:6-2:9) in which Malachi berates the priests for the laxity which he sees: they offer as sacrifice polluted food and lame animals; they "have not kept my ways" (2:9); they "have corrupted the covenant of Levi" (2:8). The way in which Malachi presents his charges is worthy of note; unlike the pre-exilic prophets, he does not use direct words of judgement, but rather the specific form of a disputation. He enters into a developed argument with the priests, beginning with the general principle which is assumed to be self-evident, "A son honors his father, and a servant his master." The language of the Hebrew text here is very close to Ex 20:12, and Deut 5:16 "Honor your father and your mother." Then, with rhetorical questions, he draws out the implications of this principle, "If I am a father, where is my honor?" The priests in turn ask, "How have we despised your name?" and the prophet goes on to list the accusations (1:7ff). Such an argument is effective only if the answer to the initial question can be assumed to be self-evident—of course God is a father. But, we should note, it is also assumed that the position of father is one which intrinsically carries some authority and demands some honor and recognition. The father expects to receive something from the son; from the son's perspective, the relationship to the father is one which involves obligation.

Malachi 2:10:

> Have we not all one father? Has not one God created us? Why then are we faithless to one another, profaning the covenant of our fathers?

Again we have a disputation passage (2:10-16) introduced by a question. The Hebrew text in verses 11-16 is extremely difficult; in fact, some commentators would judge that verse 15 is one of the most unintelligible in the whole of the Old Testament in terms of its actual meaning. For our purposes, it is enough to say that the basic issue in this dispute seems to be the prophet's denouncement of marriages with foreign wives and of divorce. Again, Malachi argues the case by stating a self-evident principle in the form of a rhetorical question, "Is there not one father for all of us?" Given the parallel question "Did not one God create us?," the one father is almost certainly God, not the patriarch Abraham. But Malachi is not espousing an early version of the liberal maxim of the "fatherhood of God and the brotherhood of man." His words are addressed specifically to the restored community in Jerusalem; to invoke the language of God as father carries with it the implication of concrete obligations to one another within the community of those who are the offspring of the same father.

Jeremiah 3:4, 3:19:

> My father, you are the friend of my youth . . . (3:4)

> I thought how I would set you among my sons,
> and give you a pleasant land,
> a heritage most beauteous of all nations.
> And I thought you would call me, My Father,
> and would not turn from following me. (3:19)

In the judgement of many commentators, the two verses quoted here are parts of a longer poem (3:1-4:4) which has been interrupted by the insertion of the prose section in verses 6-18. In verses 1-5, Israel is depicted as a wife who has been faithless to her husband "You have played the harlot with many lovers" (3:1); her wickedness defiles the land so that drought strikes. Then, in the time of calamity she bursts forth with terms of endearment, "my father," "friend of my youth." Yet God complains that these are only empty words; in terms of concrete deeds "you have done all the evil that you could" (3:5). In verse 19, God again speaks of the ideal, of how Israel is meant to act, "And I thought you would call me, My Father, and would not turn from following me." But, of course, in reality, "as a faithless wife leaves her husband so you have been faithless to me" (3:20). The whole poem is a complex interweaving of the two metaphors of husband and father. The language of father implies obligation: God invites Israel to say "my father" but, if she does so, she must turn from her apostasy.

Jeremiah 31:7-9:

> With weeping they shall come,
> and with consolations I will lead them back,
> I will make them walk by brooks of water,
> in a straight path in which they shall not stumble;
>
> for I am a father to Israel,
> and Ephraim is my first-born son.
>
> (31:9)

These verses come from the "Book of Consolation" (Jeremiah 30-33), which is probably an expanded version of Jeremiah's core message of salvation. This oracle begins with a call to praise, "Sing aloud with gladness . . . proclaim, give praise" (verse 7), followed by the graphic picture of a new Exodus in which "the blind and the lame, the woman with child and her who is in travail" (31:8) will all return to their land. The image of God as father is invoked as the climax of this poem; it is the rationale, the explanation of why God will act to restore them, "for I am a father to Israel."

Isaiah 63:16, 64:8:

> For you are our Father,
> though Abraham does not know us
> and Israel does not acknowledge us
> you, O Lord, are our Father,
> our Redeemer from of old is your name.

(63:16)

> Yet, O Lord, you are our Father,
> we are the clay and you are our potter,
> we are all the work of your hand.

(64:8)

These two passages in which the people boldly address God directly saying, "You are our Father" are part of a long communal lament in Isaiah 63:7-64:12. To understand the full impact, particularly of 64:8, we must look at the whole unit; like the communal lament psalms (such as 44, 74, and 79), this poem follows a defined liturgical movement. The lament begins with a recital of God's mighty acts in the past, particularly the deliverance of the Exodus (63:7-14); these are the grounds for hope of deliverance in the future. Then comes a description of the present situation of distress, the sense that God has totally abandoned them so that "we have become . . . like those who are not called by your name" (63:19). This is followed by the petition for help, "O that you would rend the heavens and come down," and the confession of sin (64:1-7). Then, according to the structure of a lament, comes the pivotal verse, the turning point. The key word is "yet," the adversative *waw* in Hebrew—"*yet*, O Lord, you are our Father." This is the basis of assurance and confidence, the confession of trust, the source of hope for the future, though the poem ends with a final haunting question, "Will you keep silent and afflict us sorely?" (64:12).

As with many passages in Isaiah 56-66, it is difficult to be confident of the exact historical circumstances which underlie this text. What is clear are the signs of bitter intercommunity conflict and a pervading sense that the magnificent deliverance promised by Second Isaiah has yet to come. There is some evidence to suggest that this poem is the cry of one group within the community (the Levitical priests?) who claim that another group (the Zadokite priests?) have marginalized them and denied them access to the Temple, priesthood, and leadership in the restored community (in particular, 63:18 "your people possessed your sanctuary a little while; our adversaries have trodden it down)."[3] Verse 63:16 establishes the contrast: though the patriarchial fathers Abraham and Israel (in the person of the ruling priestly group) have rejected them, yet they can appeal to their heavenly father who is on their side, "You, O Lord, are our father." Here the titles Father and Redeemer are brought together as an expression of the divine will to act with compassion.

In Conclusion:

In these later prophets, the image of God as Father is multivalent and multidimensional. In Mal 1:6, 2:10, Jer 3:4, 3:19, the language of Father is linked to the language of obligation; if Israel is to call God Father, certain obligations, a certain stance of respect, fidelity , and obedience necessarily follows. In contrast, in Jer 31:9, Isa 63:16 and 64:8, the prophet calls God Father to express trust and confidence in divine graciousness and desire to save.

[3]For a discussion of this passage in terms of a Levite-Zadokite struggle, see Paul Hanson, *The Dawn of Apocalyptic: The Historical and Sociological Roots of Jewish Apocalyptic Eschatology,* (Fortress, 1975), pp. 79-99.

As is well known, this metaphor of God as father has become extremely problematic and controversial today.[4] Many women (and men too) experience a radical sense of alienation when male metaphors are used invariably or even predominantly in speaking of God, precisely because of the very real way in which the metaphor is often de facto literalized. Although theoretically, in our heads, we know that God is spirit and thus neither male nor female, in our lived imagination God is father, therefore clearly male. And it is not only our understanding of God which is shaped by this metaphor; to use Mary Daly's famous quote, "If God is male, then the male is God": maleness becomes normative of humanity, the only true and full image of God.

Even when we are cognizant of the dangers of literalization and determine to respect the "is/is not" nature of metaphorical language, this specific metaphor raises questions of its own. The language of fatherhood functions within the contours of "patriarchy" which in feminist writing is understood both (1) as a historical social system in which authority and power belongs totally and exclusively to the father as head of the household (as exemplified in the *paterfamilias* in Roman law and some very real vestiges in the legal systems of Western society down to our own age), and (2) as a way of understanding *all* relationships in terms of a hierarchial (superior and inferior) exercise of power, which extends not just to relationships within a family, but to relationships between

---

[4]There is, of course, a vast bibliography on this topic. Three books which I have found helpful are: the early statement of the issue by Mary Daly, *Beyond God the Father*, (Beacon Press, 1973); the more moderate discussion of Celine Mangan, *Can We Still Call God "Father,"* (Michael Glazier, 1984); the discussion of metaphor and image by Sallie McFague, *Metaphorical Theology*, (Fortress, 1982), particularly chapter 5, "God the Father, model or idol?," pp. 145-194.

people of differing ages, races, classes and men and women in all situations. To say "God is father" is often viewed as the final and absolute sanction and divine legitimation of the entire patriarchial system.

Our reading of the prophetic claim "You are our father" not only shapes, but is shaped by our experience of what fatherhood means, both personally and in our culture as a whole. For some, "father" is seen in terms of power, dominance, authority; as Dorothee Soelle has said succinctly, "Male power for me, is something to do with roaring, shooting and giving orders."[5] But, as we have seen, the prophets have a quite different picture of what it is to be father. "You are my father" is an expression of trust and confidence. Precisely because God is father, we are assured God will act to save; the father metaphor is evoked specifically to describe the compassionate love of God. Many years ago (and quite apart from the recent feminist discussions of the question), the German New Testament scholar Joachim Jeremias pointed out that this understanding of father is very ancient; over three thousand years ago, the Sumerian-Babylonian god Ea was described as being "like a merciful father." Jeremias noted, "For orientals, the word 'Father,' as applied to God, thus encompasses, from earliest times, something of what the word 'Mother' signifies among us."[6] The psalmist shares this same understanding of fatherhood when he makes the comparison "as a father pities his children, so the Lord pities those who fear him" (Ps

[5]Dorothee Soelle, "Paternalistic Religion as Experienced by Woman" in *God as Father?*, edited by Johannes-Baptist Metz and Edward Schillebeeckx, Concilium 143, (Seabury Press, 1981) p. 72.

[6]Joachim Jeremias, *The Prayers of Jesus*, Studies in Biblical Theology 6, (SCM Press, 1967), p. 11.

103:13). Perhaps these prophetic texts have something to say to us today when it is so often assumed that only feminine images can express divine qualities of love, tenderness and compassion.

But the other side of the prophetic understanding of father is equally important. Malachi (1:6, 2:10) and Jeremiah (3:19) also insist that fatherhood involves a certain basic respect and honor due to the father as father—not as tyrant or hierarchial master, but as the giver of life (see Ex. 20:12; Sir 3:10-16). In our culture there is sometimes the tendency to treat God as a non-judgemental high school guidance counsellor, who lays out some options before us and remains relatively indifferent to our choices. The image of God as father calls forth that aspect of God which intrinsically demands honor and respect. To relate to God as father involves, paradoxically, not only a sense of trust in God's care, but also a recognition of what is owed.

God As Mother

One way in which the prophets help us to avoid that impoverishment and distortion of the imagination which results from the literalizing of language is by inviting us to imagine God both as father and as mother. The language of God as mother is not peculiar to the later period;[7] recall, for instance, the early poem in Deut 32:18 "you forgot the God who writhed in labor with you" (my translation; the RSV

---

[7]For a more complete study, see Virginia Ramey Mollenkott, *The Divine Feminine: The Biblical Imagery of God as Female*, (Crossroad, 1984).

reads "who gave you birth)." However, it is with Second and Third Isaiah that this image came into particular prominence.

Isaiah 42:5-17:

> For a long time I have held my peace
> I have kept still and restrained myself;
> now I will cry out like a woman in travail,
> I will gasp and pant.
>
> (Isa 42:14)

This verse is part of a longer poem, Isa 42:5-17, describing the imminent act of divine intervention. Until now, God has been silent and restrained in the face of the terrible defeat of his people; this is the moment for action; this is the time to "sing to the Lord a new song" (42:10). First, God is described in the most masculine of all images, as a conqueror going forth, a warrior ready to do battle (Isa 42:13; see pp. 85-86). Then, in a dramatic change of simile, the warrior becomes the woman in childbirth, crying out, gasping, unable to catch her breath in the pain of labor. The juxtaposition of the two images has an element of comparison as well as contrast: the giving of birth, like the waging of battle, requires the ultimate of effort.

Isaiah 66:7-16:

> As one whom his mother comforts,
> so I will comfort you;
> you shall be comforted in Jerusalem
>
> (66:13)

This extended poem, Isa 66:7-16, also takes up the metaphor of childbirth. The poem begins in careful ambiguity; "she" is in labor (66:7); suddenly, without the normal pains of childbirth, the baby is born. Only in verse 8b is the subject revealed: "for as soon as *Zion* was in labor, she brought forth her sons." Yet, verse 9 turns to disputation, voicing the questions which plague the community: why is there still delay? Why does it look as if God will shut the womb and fail to bring about this new birth? The answer is a summons to rejoice (66:10); Jerusalem is presented as a prosperous mother, rejoicing in her children. The poem reaches its climax in verse 13—the mother comforting her son, Jerusalem comforting her children, God comforting the people are all woven together. Without actually calling God mother, the poet has skilfully introduced the maternal image.

Totally apart from these incidents of specifically feminine God-language, Second Isaiah has a special sensitivity to male and female parallelism: "Woe to him who says to a father 'what are you begetting?' or to a woman 'with what are you in travail?'" (45:10); "Kings shall be your foster fathers, and their queens your nursing mothers" (49:23); "Look to your father Abraham, and to Sarah who bore you" (51:2). In a number of other passages, while not making such a bold statement as "You are my mother," Second Isaiah delights in comparisons which involve mothers, "Can a woman forget her sucking child, that she should have no compassion on the son of her womb? Even these may forget, yet I will not forget you" (Isa 49:15). If the mother should try to forget her nursing baby, the pain of her full breasts will move her to take up her child; the "even" suggests the remotest impossibility, but God's remembrance is still more certain.

Occasionally, owing to the subtleties of the language, the female imagery comes across in a slightly different and more forceful sense in Hebrew than it does in English translation. One example of this occurs just prior to the verse "Thou art our Father" which we discussed above. The people lament: "The yearning of your heart and your compassion are withheld from me" (Isa 63:15). In Hebrew, the word for compassion is *rahamin* which is derived from the root for the noun womb, *rehem*. What is described here is the purely gratuitous compassion and tenderness which link a mother to the child of her womb. While this word was used in a non-anatomical sense and could thus be applied to men (as in Ps 103:13 "as a father pities (*rahem*) his children"; or in Gen 44:30 in the case of Joseph whose *rahamin* was stirred toward his brothers), the Hebrew poet would be sensitive to the feminine nuance of the word. The God who is father is also the God who loves with the love of a mother. As Pope John Paul II recognizes in his discussion of divine mercy, "The Old Testament attributes to the Lord precisely those characteristics [of a mother] when it uses the term *rahamin* in speaking of him [sic]."[8]

In the past, we have often virtually overlooked these prophetic passages which are rich in feminine imagery for God—a God who writhes in childbirth, who nurses her child at the breast, who comforts with a mother's love. These passages are in Scripture; we just have not seen them. Our imagination has been restricted and our language of prayer and liturgy has been reduced, confined to more conventional ways of imaging the Deity. And not only our understanding of God, but also our understanding of humanity is consequently impoverished.

[8]Pope John Paul II, *Dives in Misericordia*, (Nov 13, 1980), footnote 52.

God As Warrior

Although some people are troubled by the language of God as mother (often being unaware of the scriptural warrant for it), for others a much more problematic image is that of God as warrior. For them, this is the crux, the *scandalon* (Matt 16:23) in its literal sense of a "stumbling block." How can the God revealed by Jesus, who invites us, "learn from me; for I am gentle and lowly in heart" (Matt 11:29), be the same God who puts on the armor of a warrior and marches forth to battle, exalting in the blood dripping from the sword (Isa 34:5)? It is true that Old Testament scholars will often situate such texts within the context of an ancient sacral institution which they call "holy war," but the very term "holy war" posits an untenable juxtaposition of irreconcilable opposites. It is too facile a solution to claim that this warrior picture is only a peripheral image of God from a few isolated and eccentric passages, or that it belongs solely to an early, primitive stage of biblical religon.[9] Rather, as Peter Craigie reminds us, "One of the dominant representations of God in the Old Testament is that of God as warrior."[10]

When the psalmist asks, "Who is the King of glory?" and

---

[9]In an apparent effort to mitigate the problems with this image, the American Bishops say, "This image [of the warrior God] was gradually transformed, particularly after the experience of exile . . . other images and other understandings of God's activity became predominate" (*The Challenge of Peace: God's Promise and Our Response*, A Pastoral Letter on War and peace, NCCB, 1983, #31). The texts which we have been examining do not bear out the claim that this image faded in the post-exilic period.

[10]Peter Craigie, *The Problem of War in the Old Testament*, (William Eerdmans, 1978), p. 11. Craigie's discussion is particularly perceptive as it comes from a man who came to the study of theology from the Royal Air Force.

receives the answer, "The Lord, strong and mighty, the Lord, mighty in battle" (Ps 24:8), this refrain takes us back to the Exodus which Israel understood in terms of a glorious military victory won by God. One of the earliest pieces of Hebrew poetry which has come down to us, the song of Moses, sung in exuberance and triumph after the deliverance, extols the God of the Exodus, "The Lord is a man of war; the Lord is his name" (Ex 15:3); "Thy right hand, O Lord, glorious in power, they right hand, O Lord, shatters the enemy" (15:6). In the more subdued language of the prosaic account, Moses encourages the people with the assurance, "The Lord will fight for you" (Ex 14:14). Other very early hymnody—Judges 5, Deut 33 (especially 26-29), Hab 3—likewise describes the Warrior God in the most bellicose of language. Some of the psalms carry this motif back to the very act of creation, drawing upon the common ancient Near Eastern mythological description of creation as a mighty victory by the deity over the power of chaos: "You rule the raging of the sea; when its waves rise, you still them. You crushed Rahab like a carcass, you scattered your enemies with your mighty arm" (Ps 89:9-10). Clearly, in the formative period of Israel's faith it was both important and acceptable to describe God as a victorious warrior who overthrew in battle the adversaries, both cosmic and national, thereby establishing order and peace. The image of God as warrior is found rarely in the long Deuteronomistic history and in pre-exilic prophecy. But the prophets of the exile and post-exilic times reactivated this metaphor in order to say something essential about their God. While we will be able here to look at only three specific passages, even a cursory reading of the following list of texts will give some sense of the power and centrality of this image: Isa 42:10-16, 51:9-11, 52:12, 59:15b-20, 63:1-6, 63:19-64:2, 66:15-16, Isa 34-35 (chapters from Second Isaiah or someone close to him in time and mentality), Isa 24:1-3, 27:1, Zech 9, Zech 14, Ezek 38-39 (for further discussion of many of these texts in terms of the eschatological scenario, see pp. 54-61, 145-149).

Isaiah 42:5-17:

> The Lord goes forth like a mighty man,
> like a man of war he stirs up his fury,
> he cries out, he shouts aloud;
> he shows himself mighty against his foes
>
> (42:13)

It is most instructive to pay attention to the specific form of this hymn. The introductory "sing to the Lord a new song" picks up the language of psalms 33:3, 40:3, 96:1, 98:1, 144:9. Then following the standard form for a hymn, after the summons to praise comes a statement of what God has done to call forth praise. In this poem, God's action is still to come and so, in that sense, we can talk of an "eschatological hymn." In a magnificent call to faith, the prophet invites the people to celebrate this coming act of deliverance, doing so with complete assurance for "new things I now declare; before they spring forth I tell you of them" (42:9).

Verse 13 moves to specific description of the deliverance. God "goes forth like a mighty man"; the translation here is quite literal; we could also say "a warrior." The language is purposefully reminiscent of Ex 15:3 "The Lord is a man of war" (we will be examining the Exodus links more closely in the next chapter, pp. 94-101). Phrases such as "goes forth," "his fury," "he cries out, he shouts aloud" are all technical language of warfare. Then, after the sudden change to the image of a woman giving birth (see p. 80), we have a list of verbs describing what the Divine Warrior will do. As in all this ancient poetry (Hab 3, Ps 18:6-15), when the Divine Warrior marches forth, nature is transformed: "I will lay waste mountains and hills . . . I will turn the rivers into islands" (42:15). The Exodus motif returns with the language of the "way" (42:16); finally, God who once went before them in a pillar of fire (Ex 13:21) will now again "turn the darkness before them into light" (42:16). As is typical with Second Isaiah, the poem ends with a condemnation of those who are deluded into thinking that the idols of the Babylonians have any power at all—the whole poem is an argument that power resides only with the Warrior God of Israel.

Isaiah 63:1-6:

> Who is this that comes from Edom,
> in crimsoned garments from Bozrah,
> he that is glorious in his apparel
> marching in the greatness of his strength?   (63:1)

Third Isaiah presents an almost revolting scene (replete with blood and gore) of God as a warrior, marching back from executing judgement upon the peoples of the earth, wearing garments splattered with the blood of the enemy. Even if people have never read Isaiah per se, parts of this text are suggested to their imagination by the Battle Hymn of the Republic: "He is trampling out the vintage where the grapes of wrath are stored."

The poem takes the form of a dialogue. A sentry challenges the blood-splattered warrior with the traditional question "Who is this that comes . . . ?" and receives the unequivocal response "It is I." Much of the power of the first line of this carefully crafted poetry lies in the play on the sounds of words: in Hebrew, Edom has the same consonants as the word *adum* "red"; Bozrah (the captial of Edom) sounds like *bozer* "the vintager." Edom has become a symbol of all the nations (notice "the peoples" in verses 3 and 6) who are to experience judgement on "the day of vengeance." In fact, one of the distinctive features of post-exilic prophecy is what has been called "the Damm-Edom theology!"[11] On one level, the animosity between Israel and Edom is rooted in the Jacob-Esau stories of the patriarchs (see Mal 1:2-5); historically, the hostility was flamed by the concrete involvement of the Edomites with the destruction of Jerusalem and the subsequent encroachment into Judahite territory (Ps 137:7, Obad 1:14). In texts like this (also Isa 34:6, Ezek 35:1-15), Edom has become the archetype of "the enemy," the symbol of all the forces of evil and opposition.

The second question asked by the sentinel "Why is your apparel red?" sets the stage for the extended image in verses 3-6 of the treading of the vine press and crushing of the grapes as the destruction of the peoples. Again, this is not a new image; in an even harsher application, the author of the poem in Lamentations had already applied this to God's action against his own people "The Lord has trodden as in a wine press the virgin daughter of Judah" (Lam 1:15, also Joel 3:13).

In this passage, we see prophecy developing into a more apocalyptic style—all of the foreign nations have been molded into "the peoples" and have lost their historical specificity; judgement is not within the workings of a recognized historical process. There is no human agent; on this day of vengeance God alone will be the conquering Warrior.

[11]Bruce C. Cresson, "The Condemnation of Edom in Postexilic Judaism," *The Use of the Old Testament in the New and Other Essays*, edited by J.M. Efird, (Duke University Press, 1972), pp. 125-48.

Zechariah 14:1-5:

> For I will gather all the nations against Jerusalem to battle . . .
> Then the Lord will go forth and fight against those nations as
> when he fights on a day of battle
>
> (14:2-3)

Zechariah 14 is one of the most clearly developed eschatological scenarios, and certainly one of the latest passages in
the post-exilic corpus. Human imagination is stretched to the
utmost as the prophet strains to express what is to occur "on
that day." The language is clearly militaristic throughout (note
the verbs: spoil, gather, divide, go forth, plunder, ravish, fight).
The prophet portrays God gathering the nations to do battle
against Jerusalem, a dramatic reversal of the ancient mythological theme of Ps 2, 46, and 48 where the nations amass
against Jerusalem but "as soon as they saw it, they were
astounded; they were in panic, they took to flight" (Ps 48:5).
Now, the nations gather and wreak havoc and disaster on half
of the population, while the other half escapes. It is a time of
judgement for some, salvation for others. The prophetic emphasis on the people as a whole is in the process of giving way to a
more apocalyptic distinction between the good/the evil, the
saved/ the damned. But once the nations have fulfilled their
role, the Divine Warrior turns against them. Even the topo-
graphy of the land is altered; though verse 5 is difficult, the
sense is that the valleys and mountains rearrange to form a
magnificent east-west highway, a broad processional way for
the Warrior to march victorious with the holy ones (the saved
and the angelic forces).

In Conclusion:

Having looked in some detail at three specific texts, it is

clearer why the image of God as warrior became so important in post-exilic prophecy. At a time when historical reality registered only defeat and ignominy, when God seemed powerless or at best indifferent, the prophets made bold to pronounce the daring word of assurance that God remained in control of history, still ready and able to liberate as in the days of Exodus. As part of this vision, Second Isaiah and subsequent prophets revitalized the Divine Warrior language which they had inherited from their ancestors in the faith, seeking to give expression to the conviction of God's ultimate control, even over the seemingly invincible Persian Empire. The final battle, still to come, would bring absolute victory on the Day of the Lord. God as warrior is a God of power, might, victory, and sovereignty.

For us, in our day, in a world where war has been glorified, where military spending expands every year at the expense of the needs of the poor, where nuclear warfare would mean the ultimate destruction of human life and of our planet, what do we as Christians do with these biblical passages? Is it still necessary or even possible for us to speak of God as Warrior? What does it say if we readily advocate omitting, or at least ignoring, a major part of what we call the Canon of Sacred Scripture? Clearly this is not just a theoretical question. On one level, witness the depth of feeling and furor created when the United Methodist Church's Hymnal Revision Committee in the United States recently suggested omitting the Battle Hymn of the Republic from its hymnbook because of the excessively militaristic language about God. Whatever we might think of the arguments put forth, clearly people sensed that something important was at stake (the present decision is that the hymn will be included!). There is still much work which needs to be done, both on the level of empirical research and of theoretical reflection, on the relationship between our images of God and our stance on issues of war and peace. Recently, I have heard it suggested that one reason why many Catholic priests and religious are able to admit the possibility of war within a Christian framework (as in the traditional "just war" theory) is that their spirituality is nurtured on daily reading of the psalms in the Liturgy of the Hours and thus, repeated exposure to the image of God as warrior. A similar type of correlation is perhaps reflected in a famous statement attributed to the biblical theologian, George E. Wright, during the height of the Vietnam war; in answer to the increasingly vocal peace movement, Wright is alleged to have responded, "Yahweh was no pacifist, nor am I."

To image God as warrior is potentially dangerous. Yet *this is* a biblical image. For my part, I can give no easy answer as to how it is to be fitted into, or omitted from, our spirituality. But let me close with two final thoughts in this connection. At this point, the discussion has led us back again to our initial reflections on the nature of God-language. A metaphorical statement, "God is a man of war" by definition cannot be absolutized, as if it provides a literal description or an ethical norm. This is quite simply giving way to the temptation to treat metaphor uncritically and unreflectively, to force it to be what it cannot be. Secondly, in our day, given the horror of the wars of this century and the spectre of the possible annihilation of human life, if we judge that the biblical image of God as warrior should be abandoned, we are left, as individuals and as a community, with some serious questions—What other language and imagery might capture for us the aspect of the divine power and might? What other language and imagery will call us to ultimate trust and confidence in the final divine victory over the forces of evil and chaos?

4

THE OLD AND THE NEW

Behold, I am doing a new thing

(Isa 43:19)

The Exile marked a time of ending and a time of new beginning, a time of death and a time of re-creation. As we have already noted, the shock of loss and dislocation was real and overwhelming. It found expression in powerful words of complaint and lament: "The Lord has forsaken me, my Lord has forgotten me" (Isa 49:14); "The way of the Lord is not just" (Ezek 18:25, 33:17); "My soul is bereft of peace, I have forgotten what happiness is" (Lam 3:17). But soon there were also voices which directed attention to the future rather than the past, voices which were confident that God's final word had not yet been spoken. At first this expectation was inchoate and tentative, the simple trust that something new was to come:

> The steadfast love of the Lord never ceases,
> his mercies never come to an end;
> they are new every morning;
> great is your faithfulness.

(Lam 3:22-23)

91

It was the task of the prophets, Jeremiah, Ezekiel and especially Second Isaiah, to expound the concrete working out of this new action in the realm of history.

For these prophets, the new was inexorably linked with the old; they believed that it was in remembering the past that the future could be recognized. Throughout the Old Testament, remembrance is a sacred duty and obligation. The people are commanded "you shall *remember* that you were a servant in the land of Egypt" (Deut 5:15); "you shall *remember* what the Lord your God did to Pharaoh and to all Egypt" (Deut 7:18); *remember* the word which Moses the servant of the Lord commanded you" (Josh 1:13). This remembering is not just an intellectual activity, a way of accumulating and possessing information. It is a remembering which takes place most fully in ritual and in celebration, above all in that great communal act of remembrance, the annual celebration of the feast of Passover—"this day shall be for you a memorial day" (Ex 12:14). In the celebration of this feast, the very act of remembering made the events of the Exodus living and available, not only to the generation which historically experienced them, but to each subsequent generation. Throughout the ages right up until today, when the Jewish family gathers for the Seder supper, when the ritual is celebrated, the four questions asked, and Passover story (*Haggadah*) retold, this is an act of remembrance which makes the Exodus a living reality:

> In every generation, every person should feel as though he had gone forth from Egypt . . . not only our ancestors alone did the Holy One redeem but *us* as well, along with them.[1]

[1] A *Passover Haggadah*, edited by Herbert Bronstein, The Central Conference of American Rabbis, 1974, pp. 56-57.

Such memory is based upon and rooted in tradition. It is a communal memory which evokes what God has done for *the people*, not just for individuals. It is this memory and tradition which enables us to make sense of the present. As Tevye sings in *Fiddler on the Roof*: "Tradition, tradition, that's what makes us what we are." But even more, the memory of what God has done in the past is the indispensable foundation for confidence that God can act in the future.

But true as this may be, it is also true that tradition and memory are dangerous and ambivalent concepts. In recent years, we have seen attitudes toward tradition fluctuate dramatically, both religiously and culturally. First we experienced the almost nihilistic mood of much of North American culture in the 1960s, when tradition was scorned and everything had to begin anew with "me and my experience." Then the pendulum swung back in the late 1970's; as a phenomenon such as the reaction to the book and the TV program *Roots* attested, people discovered, somewhat to their surprise, that there can be a positive value in a knowledge of the past, in remembering the place "where I have been." This cultural phenomenon has been paralleled by much that has happened in the Church. With somewhat childish euphoria in the immediate aftermath of Vatican II, some Catholics acted as if it were possible to deny 2000 years of history and begin *de nouveau*; now many of these same people are experiencing afresh the power of tradition and memory in establishing and shaping a sense of rootedness and identity. It is tradition which can save us from being a chameleon church, entirely at the mercy of changing cultural and social mores. As the modern philosopher Gadamer noted, "To stand within a tradition does not limit the freedom of

Knowledge but makes it possible."[2] Yet Gadamer's observation also contains a hint of warning. Tradition can be, and often has been, experienced as limiting and confining, a means of locking us into the past and predetermining the future. Then tradition functions only as a yoke and a restraint on creativity and imagination; it has nothing to say except "that's not how it was done before."

We are not the first to recognize the multivalent nature of memory and tradition. The same prophet who exhorted the people to "remember the former things of old" (Isa 46:9) also admonished them to "remember not the former things, nor consider the things of old" (Isa 43:18). As we begin our reflection on tradition the paradox of these two prophetic commands stands before us as a salutary caution. In this chapter, we want to consider how the post-exilic prophets listened to, reshaped and, at times, totally inverted the traditions which they inherited from the past. Our reflection on their use of tradition holds the promise of offering some guidance to our culture and our church as we struggle both to be faithful to the traditions which we have inherited and to take possession of them in a way which makes for freedom and creativity.

The Exodus Tradition In Second Isaiah

Central to the heritage of the later prophets was the living memory of what God had done for Israel when they were slaves in Egypt—a memory of oppression, of crying out to God, of deliverance and freedom. In a multitude of ways, this

---

[2]Hans-Georg Gadamer, *Truth and Method* (Seabury, 1975), p. 324.

tradition had formed the living core of Israel's profession of faith throughout the centuries. For example, in the first commandment, God was identified thus: "I am the Lord your God who brought you out of the land of Egypt" (Ex 20:2, Deut 5:6). When the first fruits of the harvest were presented before the Lord, a formula was to be recited, encapsulating key elements of the Exodus experience: "A wandering Aramean was my father; and he went down into Egypt and sojourned there . . . and the Egyptians treated us harshly and afflicted us . . . then we cried to the Lord the God of our fathers, and the Lord heard our voice . . . and the Lord brought us out of Egypt with a mighty hand and and outstretched arm . . ." (Deut 26:5-9). Solemn oaths were sworn according to the formula, "As the Lord lives, who brought up the people of Israel out of the land of Egypt" (Jer 16:14). "When your son asks you in time to come" about the meaning of the laws and ordinances, this formative story is to be told: "We were Pharoah's slaves in Egypt; and the Lord brought us out of Egypt with a mighty hand . . ." (Deut 6:20).

Thus, from the very beginning, the Exodus story constituted the basic pattern for deliverance and provided the mold in which other stories of deliverance and salvation could be cast. So it was that the crossing of the Jordan River into the Promised Land was recollected as a reenactment of that paradigmatic event of deliverance: Joshua was the new Moses (Joshua 3:7); the waters split into two like walls and the people walked through dryshod (3:9-17); the time was Passover (5:10-11). Similarly, the pre-exilic prophets made frequent appeal to the memory of Exodus (e.g. Amos 2:10, 3:1; Hos 11:1, 13:4; Mic 6:4; Isa 10:24-26, 11:15-16). For Hosea, for instance, Exodus was not only a historical reminiscence, but the grounds for hope that after judgement God might lead this people back into the wilderness and "speak tenderly to her" once more (Hos 2:14).

For Second Isaiah, Exodus was not so much a memory from the past as a window on the future; that is, it had an eschatological, a "yet-to-come" dimension. Exodus language and imagery, in phrases and verses too numerous even to list, abound in the fifteen chapters of Second Isaiah.[3] I have chosen, somewhat arbitrarily, Isa 43:16-21 as our starting point:

> Thus says the Lord,
> who makes a way in the sea,
> a path in the mighty waters.
> who brings forth chariot and horse,
> army and warrior . . .
> I will make a way in the wilderness
> and rivers in the desert.
> The wild beasts will honor me,
> the jackals and the ostriches;
> for I give water in the wilderness,
> rivers in the desert,
> to give drink to my chosen people,
> the people whom I formed for myself
> that they might declare my praise.
>
> (Isa 43:16-17, 19, 21)

The Lord who once made a way in the sea (43:16) will now make "a way in the wilderness" (43:19). This imge (note also 42:16, 48:17, 49:11, 51:10), of the *way* (or the "highway" as it

---

[3]For a fuller discussion of Exodus language and typology, see the following (among many resources): B. Anderson, "Exodus Typology in Second Isaiah," *Israel's Prophetic Heritage: Essays in Honor of James Muilenburg*, eds. B.B. Anderson and W. Harrelson (SCM, 1962), pp. 177-95; M. Fishbane, "The Exodus Motif: The Paradigm of Historical Renewal," *Text & Texture: Close Readings of Selected Biblical Texts* (Schocken Books, 1979), pp. 121-40; *Exodus: A Lasting Paradigm*, eds. Bas Van Iersel and A. Weiler, Concilium 189, (T & T Clarke, 1987).

is sometimes called) harks back to the very first words of this prophet. In Isa 40:3 the heavenly voice proclaims in a powerful parallel statement using the poetic devise of chiasmus:

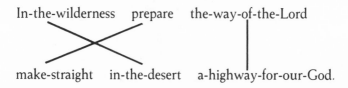

In-the-wilderness   prepare   the-way-of-the-Lord

make-straight   in-the-desert   a-highway-for-our-God.

It is surely not by chance that the final oracle of this prophet (although not employing the precise word *way*) paints a picture of the people being led upon this road in joy and peace, while even the mountains and hills burst forth in song (55:12). Isaiah's assurance that God is about to prepare a highway for the trek back from Babylon to their own land holds meaning and hope for the people precisely because they already knew that God had made a way through the Red Sea and through the parched desert in the time of the Wanderings.

But, in addition to the rich nuance which surrounded the term from the biblical tradition, the exiles had also seen for themselves the magnificent processional streets of Marduk in Babylon. From archaeology and from Babylonian hymnic texts, we can reconstruct a picture of these great processional highways in which richly robed statues of Marduk and the other gods were carried in solemn ceremony and splendor at the annual festivals. Now, there is to be "a highway for *our God*," and along it "the glory of *the Lord* [not Marduk] shall be revealed" to all flesh (40:4-5). Thus, an image already established in tradition takes on an added dimension from the contemporary experience of the exiles in Babylon.

In addition to the way, there shall be "water in the wilderness, rivers in the desert (43:20). Again, the exiles knew, both from the tradition of the desert Wanderings, and from their own life-experience, that without water the desert is a place of death. In the first Exodus, God had intervened at points of crisis to heal the bitter waters of Marah (Ex 15:22-25) and to make water burst forth from the rock at Rephidim (Ex 17:1-7). But now, the desert will have permanent rivers "to give drink to my chosen people" (Isa 43:20, 41:18). "The new thing" will surpass the old. In this new Exodus, even the animal world will be included, "the wild beasts will honor me, the jackals and the ostriches" (43:20). This is not the language of zoology and history; the new dispensation requires the language of poetry. The conclusion of the poem names the purpose of this deliverance—the formation of a people "to declare my praise" (43:21). As at the first Exodus when "Moses and the people of Israel sang this song to the Lord" (Ex 15:1-18) and "Miriam the prophetess, the sister of Aaron, took a timbrel in her hand; and all the women went out after her with timbrels and dancing" (Ex 15:20), so now song and praise can be the only fitting response. In anticipation, the prophet has already burst forth in an eschatological hymn, "Sing to the Lord a new song, his praise from the end of the earth" (42:10).

Certain other key Exodus motifs can be found in Isa 52:11-12:

> Depart, depart go out thence,
> touch no unclean thing;
> go out from the midst of her,
> purify yourselves,
> you who bear the vessels of the Lord.
> For you shall not go out in haste,
> and you shall not go in flight,
> for the Lord will go before you,
> and the God of Israel will be your rear guard.

In his mind's eye, the prophet has placed himself already in Jerusalem and charges the exiles to leave Babylon, "Depart, depart, go out thence" (52:11). As priests in a state of cultic purity once led the procession through the Wilderness carrying the ark, so now the people are charged to be purified ("touch no unclean thing") as they carry back the sacred vessels of the Lord. These vessels of the First Temple, carted off as booty by Nebuchadnezzar (2 Kgs 25:13-17), and restored at the explicit decree of the Persian king (Ezra 6:5) serve as a powerful symbol of continuity between the old and the new. In the first Exodus, the fugitives had prepared in haste, "your loins girded, your sandals on your feet, and your staff in your hand; and you shall eat it in haste" (Ex 12:11; also Deut 16:13); now, in a conscious reversal (using the exact same rare Hebrew word for "haste"), Second Isaiah commands, "you shall not go out in haste" (52:12) The ignominious element of speed in the first Exodus is totally erased in the second, as again the new supersedes the old. In both, "the Lord will go before you, and the God of Israel will be your rear guard" (52:12b; compare Ex 13:21-22, 14:19-20).

Three elements—cosmos, history, future—come together in the final Exodus passage to which we turn our attention, Isa 51:9-11:

> Awake, awake, put on strength,
> O arm of the Lord;
> awake, as in the days of old,
> the generations of long ago.
> Was it not you that cut Rahab in pieces,
> that pierced the dragon?
> Was it not you that dried up the sea,
> the waters of the great deep;
> that made the depths of the sea a way

> for the redeemed to pass over?
> And the ransomed of the Lord shall return,
> and come to Zion with singing;
> everlasting joy shall be upon their heads;
> they shall obtain joy and gladness,
> and sorrow and sighing shall flee away.

In this direct address to the arm of the Lord personified, we are meant to hear an echo of the Exodus refrain, "The Lord brought you out with a mighty hand and an outstretched arm." This is the Divine Warrior, "the man of war" who triumphed over the sea (Ex 15:3). But Second Isaiah boldly takes us back even beyond the Exodus to the cosmic battle of the Lord with the sea monster, the force of chaos: "Was it not you that cut Rahab in pieces, that pierced the dragon?" (51:9). Here the prophet draws upon ancient mythological traditions preserved in the cult (compare Ps 74:13-14, 89:10, also Job 26:12), combining these with the historic Exodus tradition to give a glimpse into the shape of the future—the God who has acted in creation and in history is surely able to act now so that "the ransomed of the Lord shall return, and come to Zion with singing" (51:11).

In Conclusion:

Second Isaiah could turn to Exodus language precisely because there was an experiential point of contact between the conditions of the people in Egypt who cried to the Lord "because of their broken spirit and their cruel bondage" (Ex 6:9), and the conditions of the people in Babylon who cried out, "The Lord has forsaken me, my Lord has forgotten me" (Isa 49:19). The God who answered then would speak again in this new situation. Because its potential as a vehicle of revelation was not exhausted at the Red Sea, Exodus could continue to function as a "type," the full realization of which still lay in the future.

We must take care that talking boldly of Exodus-as-type does not seduce us into a static understanding, as if knowledge of past tradition can guarantee for us the potentialities of the future. A seeming grasp of tradition can too easily constrict our vision, allowing us to blithely assure ourselves that the future, if not in our grasp, is at least rendered manageable within the strictures provided by memory. As T.S. Elliot challenged us "to care and not to care," likewise we are summoned "to remember and not to remember." In Babylon, memory alone could have blocked the people from an openness to totally new dimensions of divine activity. Nothing in the memory of the Exodus from Egypt prepared the people for Cyrus—for the fact that God would choose as "his anointed," not a member of the chosen people, but a pagan, a worshipper of false gods. Yet it is of Cyrus, the Persian, that the Lord said "He is my shepherd, and he shall fulfill all my purpose" (44:28). The God of surprises bursts forth beyond the limits of memory and the expectations of tradition: "Behold, I am doing a new thing; now it springs forth, do you not perceive it?" (43:19).

The Exodus Tradition In Ezekiel

Gershom Scholem reminds us that tradition is "infinitely interpretable."[4] Second Isaiah did not, of course, exhaust the meaning of Exodus. To demonstrate this we need only to call

[4]Gershom G. Scholem, *The Messianic Idea in Judaism and Other Essays on Jewish Spirituality*, (Schocken Books, 1971), p 295.

to mind how the language of Exodus was taken up in a radically new way by the early Christians where it provided a vocabulary and a paradigm to speak about Jesus's passion and death as a new "exodus" (Lk 9:31), about Baptism (1 Cor 10:1-4) and the remission of sins (Romans 6:15-19). Even among the prophets, Second Isaiah was not alone in recognizing the potential for a creative appropriation and reinterpretation of this fundamental motif.

The prophet Ezekiel takes up the Exodus motif, but in a very different, even shocking manner in chapter 20. Precisely because this section might not be particularly familiar (it is not among the few "quotable quotes" of Ezekiel), it merits our examination as a fascinating example of the "infinite inter-pretability" of even the most basic tradition. (Chapters 16 and 23 can also be read as powerful reinterpretations of tradition, although we will not be able to treat them specifically here).

The incident related in chapter 20 is dated to August 14, 591 BC. The elders come to Ezekiel "to inquire of the Lord" but the nature of the request is never clearly spelled out; on the basis of the answer (finally given in verse 32), it has been speculated that they came regarding some sort of reestab-lishment of cultic worship (probably to build an altar rather than an image of the Lord). The response to their question involves a basic retelling of the whole of salvation history: the period in Egypt and the deliverance (20:5-10), the first wilder-ness generation (20:11-17), the second generation in the wilderness (20:18-26), the time in the land (20:27-31) and the centuries up to the time of exile (20:33-44). However, this telling of the story is unlike any other in the Scriptures! The tradition is treated with a radical freedom. God's election of Israel and the promise of the land is made, not to the patriarchs but to the people when they are in Egypt, "I swore to the seed of the house of Jacob, making myself known to them in the land of Egypt" (20:5). Then comes the surprising injunction to abandon "the idols of Egypt," a command which was not obeyed, "but they rebelled against me and would not listen to me" (20:8). This is a totally different remembering of the time in Egypt; only Joshua 24:14 hints of the Egyptian sojourn as a period of idolatry and worship of false gods. According to Ezekiel, the wrathful God would have destroyed them, but exercised restraint "for the sake of my name, that it should not be profaned in the sight of the nations among whom they dwelt" (20:9). God does bring the people out of Egypt in an unwilling Exodus imposed on them lest He be shamed before the nations. In a very schematized and generalized way, Ezekiel recounts the rebellion of the first generation (with particular emphasis, at least in the final edited form of the text, on the profanation of the Sabbath, 20:13, 16, 21). Even before they enter the promised Land, the Lord swears in an oath, "I swore to them in the wilderness that I would scatter them among the nations and disperse them through the countries" (20:23). In one of the most shocking statements of the Old Testament, God is even "credited" with the law demanding child sacrifice (20:26). Only after this lengthy historical survey does Ezekiel reply to the elders, with what is basically a non-answer from God, "I will not be inquired of by you" (20:31). Ezekiel looks in guarded terms to a new Exodus, "I will bring you out from the peoples and gather you from the countries where you are scattered" (20:34), but such deliverance is only to face a new period of judgement in the desert; they will return to the Lord not with joy and exaltation, but with loathing and shame for all their evils (20:43).

Surely this is a strange reversal of the whole tradition of salvation history *(Heilsgeschichte)*. Exodus has become an act of wrath, not of grace; instead of crying to the Lord for release, the people cling to the idols of Egypt; the whole series of events which Israel normally remembered as proof of God's graciousness becomes instead unholy history (*Unheilsgesichte*). It is Ezekiel's reading of the present situation combined with his theological understanding of the divine nature which led to this radical reinterpretation. Ezekiel is unmitigatedly harsh in his evaluation of his own generation, his fellow exiles; they are sinful through and through, defying God's will, succumbing to apostasy and idolatry. But, he explains, this is only to be expected: it has been so since day one, since the time in Egypt. The apostasy of that generation was punished in the Wilderness; the apostasy of this generation will also be punished. The second factor shaping Ezekiel's reading of the Exodus story is his radical sense of divine sovereignty and holiness: God is in no way able to be manipulated, or forced to respond to human action and evil. The Exodus is above all an act of divine initiative and self-manifestation: "I did it that they might know that I am the Lord" (20:20, also 20:26).

Ezekiel 20 is an example of how a specific understanding of the present as well as a fundamental theological stance both shape and in turn are shaped by the remembrance of the past. There is a dialectic between past and present. It is not only that the past influences the future; the present also determines how we read the past. We want to ask, "Who was *right* in the reading of the Exodus story—was it Ezekiel or was it Second Isaiah?" Only when we realize that this is a non-question have we begun to sense how these prophets could freely and creatively approach tradition.

Other Traditions: Abraham And Noah

Although the Exodus story served as the paradigm for Second Isaiah in his vision of the *magnalia dei* which were soon to come, the prophet says surprisingly little about the next major element in traditional salvation history. We find no clear allusions to Moses, Sinai, the making of the covenant or the giving of the law (except perhaps the rather vague reference "O that you had hearkened to my commandments!" Isa 48:18). Yet earlier prophets had fashioned a link between Exodus and Covenant; they had drawn upon standard Sinaitic covenant language (e.g. "for you are not my people and I am not your God" Hos 1:8) and had found in Moses a model for shaping their understanding of the prophetic vocation.

Although modern biblical theology has tended to see covenant, meaning specifically the Sinai covenant, as the central core of Israel's religious experience, the tradition knew of other and very different covenants, covenants made with Noah, Abraham, David, even Phinehas (Num 25:1-18) and the Levites (Jer 33:19-22). In these instances, God enters into an agreement which is much more in the nature of a promise which is unconditional, rather than a contract which is spelled out in terms of obligations on the part of both parties. These convenants will not be rendered null or the promises void even in the face of the worst imaginable violations. The focus is on the eternal fidelity of God whose promise will endure forever: to Noah, "The waters shall never again become a flood to destroy all flesh" (Gen 9:15); to Abraham, "I will make you exceedingly fruitful; and I will make nations of you" (Gen 17:6); to David, "And your house and your kingdom shall be made sure for ever before me; your throne shall be established for ever" (2 Sam 7:16). In each case, this is an "everlasting covenant," not dependent on the fidelity of the human agent: "If his children forsake my law and do not walk according to my ordinances, if they violate my statutes and do not keep my commandments, then I will punish their transgression with the rod and their iniquity with scourges; but I will not remove from him my steadfast love, or be false to my faithfulness. I will not violate my covenant, or alter the word that went forth from my lips" (Ps 89:30-34). Precisely how the tradition held in tension two very different understandings about covenant (covenant as condition and covenant as promise) is a difficult question, though not our main concern here.[5]

Abraham and Noah

When we retell the story of salvation history, we tend to begin with Abraham, "our father in faith." Yet the pre-exilic prophets (in those oracles commonly judged to be authentic to them) make no reference to Abraham or to the covenant established with him, but begin their narration of salvation history with the deliverance from Egypt and the journey to Sinai (for instance, Mic 6:3-5). Ezekiel introduces a single brief reference to Abraham in the specific context of polemic about the right to possess the land in the turmoil of the Exile (Ezek 33:24). Thus, we are startled to hear Second Isaiah call upon the memory of Abraham and of Sarah (incidentally, the only mention of Sarah outside the book of Genesis):

[5]For a helpful discussion of some of the basic issues involved, see Jon D. Levenson, "The Davidic Covenant and Its Modern Interpreters," *Catholic Biblical Quarterly*, 41, 1979, pp. 205-19.

Hearken to me
you who pursue deliverance,
you who seek the Lord;
look to the rock from which you were hewn,
and to the quarry from which you were digged.
Look to Abraham your father
and to Sarah who bore you;
for when he was but one I called him,
and I blessed him and made him many.

(Isa 51:1-2)

As God took Abraham "when he was but one" and made of him a mighty nation, so can God do for the remnant of the nation now in exile; the divine fidelity to the promise to Abraham is the basis of hope in this new situation. Also, in Isa 41:8, the exiles are addressed as "Israel, my servant, Jacob, whom I have chosen, the offspring of Abraham, my friend" (literally, in Hebrew, "the one who loves me")." This poignant epithet "the one who loves me" (found also in 2 Chron 20:7) is again a reminder of enduring love stretching back to the first ancestor.

But Second Isaiah looks back even further than Abraham as he seeks to ground his vision of hope in the experience of the past. In a beautiful poem in 54:1-17, he addresses Zion in the figure of a barren woman. In a magnificent reversal, she who has known the curse of barrenness and humiliation is summoned to rejoice, "Sing, O barren one, who did not bear; break forth into singing and cry aloud, you who have not been in travail! For the children of the desolate one will be more than the children of her that is married, says the Lord" (54:1). In a second image, she who has been divorced and cast off is reclaimed and loved, "For a brief moment I forsook you, but with great compassion I will gather you" (54:7). The boldness to dare to believe that "with everlasting love I will have compassion on you" (54:8) comes from recalling the tradition of Noah:

For this is like the days of Noah to me
as I swore that the waters of Noah
should no more go over the earth,
so I have sworn that I will not be angry with you
and will not rebuke you.

(54:9)

Even in their worse moments of despair, the exiles have in fact experienced the fidelity of the Lord to this promise: the waters have never flooded the earth. Even as the people experience the curses which come with the violation of the Mosaic covenant (defeat by the enemy, loss of the land, exile), the remembrance of the promise to Noah at the very dawn of history still offers access to the "everlasting" nature of the divine fidelity. The Lord still loves with "everlasting love" (54:8); the joy of the redeemed is to be everlasting (51:11). Israel is saved with "everlasting salvation" (45:17); for, the word of the Lord "will stand for ever" (40:8).

Second Isaiah is indeed like the "householder who brings out of his treasure what is new and what is old" (Matt 13:52). The traditions of the covenant with Abraham and Noah which had lain dormant for centuries, overlooked by even the pre-exilic prophets, are now revived and brought forth to bring a word of life to a new historical situation. Every tradition does not need to speak to every generation. At any given time, some traditions are very relevant, some seem totally irrelevant. As we noted earlier, in much of contemporary life and theology (particularly in Liberation Theology coming from Latin America), the Exodus tradition is extensively explored and found to be rich with potential and promise, while other parts of the Scriptures—the book of Chronicles, for instance—seem totally without relevance. Yet, last century, particularly in Roman Catholicism, Chronicles (or Paralipomenon, as it was better known from its Greek title) with its emphasis on the kingship of David, the established order, and the centrality of cult, was a powerful force in shaping both religious and cultural imagination. Too often we suffer from a short-sighted point of view which would judge every tradition by its immediate and readily-apparent relevance to us *now*. Perhaps we must learn to hand on tradition, patiently and faithfully, recognizing that what might be closed to us now might again become pregnant with life and meaning in the hands of new prophets in the days to come.

The Promises To David

As we conclude this section, let us look briefly at Second Isaiah's treatment of the complex of traditions concerned with the eternal promises made to the line of David. To the exiles in Babylon, the promise that "I will establish his line for ever and his throne as the days of the heavens" (Ps 89:29) seemed to be vitiated by the harsh reality of what had just happened in history—there no longer was a Davidic king. Later, for a brief time, certain of the prophets seemed to expect these promises to find fulfillment in a concrete historical personage, Zerubbabel, to whom Haggai and Zechariah boldly applied such suggestive royal Davidic terms as "signet ring" (Hag 2:23) and "branch" (Zech 3:8, see also 4:6-10, 6:9-15). Such hopes for a literal and immediate restoration of the Davidic line quickly came to naught, and Zerubabbel faded into oblivion, though other voices in the prophetic tradition kept alive the yearning for a successor to the line of David (Ezek 34, 37:15-28, Jer 23:5-6, 33:14-26). Over the next centuries such passages fostered the hope of a "Messiah," an anointed one still to come from the line of David.

At the very time when questions about kingship would have been asked in their starkest form, Second Isaiah appropriates the Davidic tradition, but with surprising freedom. He fosters no hope that a member of the Davidic family will reclaim the throne. As we have already seen, Second Isaiah does not hesitate to take up royal terms and apply them, not to a Davidite, but to the pagan king Cyrus; it is *he* who is the Lord's anointed, the one of whom it is said, "He is my shepherd, and he shall fulfill all my purpose." (Isa 44:28, 45:1). The one specific mention of David comes in a poem at the very end of this collection, Isa 55:1-5:

> Ho, every one who thirsts,
> come to the waters;
> and he who has not money,
> come, buy and eat!
> Come, buy wine and milk
> without money and without price . . .
> Incline your ear, and come to me;
> hear, that your soul may live;
> and I will make with you
> an everlasting covenant,
> my steadfast, sure love for David.
>
> (55:1, 3)

This is a summons to a magnificent banquet (compare Prov 9:1-6, Sir 24:19-22 where Lady Wisdom invites all to share in the richness of her fare), a banquet of "what is good" given so that "your soul may live" (55:2-3). It is within this context that the divine promise is given: "I will make with you an everlasting covenant, my steadfast, sure love for David" (55:3). Contrary to every appearance, the permanent, everlasting covenant made with David is to endure, but now the covenant will be with "you"—in Hebrew this is clearly a plural pronoun. As David was "a witness to the peoples" (55:4) in that his victories over the nations testified to them of the power of the Lord rather than of their gods (Ps 18:43-45a), now it is the whole people who are to be witnesses to the nations ("you are my witnesses" Isa 43:10, 44:8). The steadfast sure love (2 Sam 7:15, Ps 89:28) granted to the Davidic line is now for all. This has been called, to use modern terminology, "a democratized form of the royal ideology";[6] be that as it may, what is certain is that Isaiah has again turned to an old tradition and adapted it in a radical and creative way to give hope to the entire people.

"And The Prophets, Do They Live Forever?" (Zech 1:5)

To this point, we have explored some of the ways in which the prophets appropriated various elements of the common tradition of their people as they called upon the past to speak a new word for the future. However, in addition to this creative reshaping of major components of the tradition (Exodus, Abraham, Noah, David), the later prophets turned specifically to the actual words and collections of the oracles from the "former prophets" (Zech 1:4). This distinctive feature of

[6]Frank Moore Cross, *Canaanite Myth & Hebrew Epic: Essays on the History of the Religion of Israel*, (Harvard University Press, 1973), p. 263.

post-exilic prophecy—the appropriation and reapplication of earlier prophetic texts—is particularly notable in Third Isaiah, Joel, Zech 9-14, and Isa 24-27. Frequently the whole phenomenon has been evaluated quite negatively. These later prophets are judged as no longer speaking a fresh word from the Lord; they are considered as weak imitators or, even worst, stale copyists of their predecessors. From this perspective, the distinctive style of prophecy which evolved in these centuries is often taken as proof of "the drying up of inspiration," and confirmation of the fact that prophecy was by this time "on its last leg." However, there is a more positive way of approaching this material. Though it might not deserve high marks for originality, this type of composition does attest to the fact that the words of the earlier prophets were already seen to be "canonical"—that is, having some sort of authoritative stature and enduring value.

We can recall that, at the same time as prophets such as Third Isaiah, Deutero-Zechariah and the author of the Isaiah Apocalypse were active, the oracles of the earlier prophets were in the process of being collected and edited in the form which we now have them. Though we know much less than we would like about the actual details of *who* was doing this and *how,* the more important and fundamental question to ask is—*why* would anyone have collected the words of prophets who had lived and spoken some two or three hundred years previously? Given, for instance, that Amos was called to speak God's word announcing "the end has come" upon the northern kingdom in the eighth century, and that he did just that, and that what he spoke took place—why continue to preserve and pronounce his words in the fifth century? Note that this is, in essence, the same fundamental question which we ask today: how can the words of a prophet like Ezekiel, spoken in 600

BC, be meaningful or significant to us some twenty-five centuries later? In the fifth century BC as in the twentieth century AD, it was not immediately self-evident that "the former prophets" were in any way relevant, apart from being a historical curiosity from a past age.

Within the prophetic corpus, this concern is handled in a number of different ways. A book like Amos, for example, was expanded by an addition, a few short verses appended in 9:11-15 which served to transform how the entire book was to be read. These two salvation oracles, the first promising "in that day" the restoration of "the booth of David which is fallen" (Amos 9:11) and the second describing the future ("behold the days are coming" 9:13) in terms of fertility and prosperity, use language and imagery which is remarkably similar to other post-exilic salvation oracles (most especially Joel 4:18, Isa 65:21-22). By this addition Amos's words of judgement, which in a sense are over and done with, are given a new function; they can now serve as an enduring admonition in a context where the final fulfillment of salvation still lies in the future. Thus, these final verses are not just a superficial imposition of "roses and lavender" upon the "blood and iron"[7] of the rest of the book; rather, when these verses are appended, the entire book is rendered usable for every generation as the words of judgement are reapplied in their situation.

But it is not only by way of an addition of new material that the words of the earlier prophets are made to live in subsequent centuries. Often there is a very specific word, phrase, or motif which is take up from an earlier text and reworked by a later prophet in a conscious and intentional manner. The purpose

[7]This is a well-known remark of Wellhausen, quoted by B. Childs, *Introduction to the Old Testament as Scripture*, (Fortress, 1979), p. 405.

was to sound an echo of the old in the new prophetic word—
but often we today entirely miss the point simply because we
do not know the Scriptures well enough to recognize spon-
taneously when an earlier text is being alluded to or quoted!
To give just two brief and simple examples of this specific type
of reapplication. We have already seen (pp. 94-101) how
Second Isaiah drew upon language and some motifs from the
Exodus tradition, and specifically the image of the way or
highway. "In the wilderness, prepare the way of the Lord" (Isa
40:3). Third Isaiah uses the exact same phrase "Build up, build
up, prepare the way" (Isa 57:14). This is not just a slavish
repetition of an earlier text because the prophet could not
think of anything new or creative. The reader in fifth century
Palestine was meant to recall the words of the prophet of the
Exile, but at the same time to recognize a slight nuance in the
use of the term. In Third Isaiah, this is not a physical
geographical road from one place to another (as from Babylon
to Palestine in Second Isaiah) but the way has become a more
metaphorical "way of salvation." Or again, compare Second
Isaiah, "The Lord will go before you and the God of Israel will
be your rear guard" (52:12) with Third Isaiah, "Your righteousness shall go before you, the glory of the Lord shall be
your rear guard" (58:8). The latter is obviously drawing upon
the former. Again, in Third Isaiah there is no real journey; the
phrase has been reinterpreted to describe the nature of the
salvation to come when the true fast of justice and release from
oppression (58:1-7) has been observed. Examples like this
could be multiplied at length showing how the later prophets
creatively used and transformed the actual words and phrases
of "the former prophets."

With other prophetic books the process was much more
complex than simply the straightforward addition of a few

concluding verses or the refashioning of a short phrase. In a book like Micah—or Jeremiah even more so—subsequent expansions of an earlier core text, editorial glosses and comments, and the addition of some totally new material are interwoven into the words of the earlier prophets in such a way that it is virtually impossible to recover the original prophetic text. Nor should we be misled into thinking that if we somehow could have the guaranteed "original words," we then would have true prophecy. It is in this very process of editing, a process which we can understand or recover only imperfectly, that the spirit of prophecy was operative in these centuries.

In this way, these later prophets became more like "learned men," more like the scribes and sages of later tradition who did not speak a new word of revelation from the Lord but who drew out, reinterpreted and reapplied the existing words of a text which was held as fixed and sacred. Perhaps something of this is reflected in the saying in later Jewish tradition: "The spirit of the prophet passed on to the sages." In some ways, these post-exilic prophets stand closer to our situation than do the earlier prophets. Is not this what we, in our day, are called to do—to ponder the words of "the former prophets" as we have them in the text of Scripture, to reinterpret and apply them anew in our generation so that, in this sense, we can answer affirmatively Zechariah's question, "And the prophets, do they live forever?" (Zech 1:5)?

5

TO ACT JUSTLY

> What does the Lord require of you but to do justice, and to love
> kindness, and to walk humbly with your God?
>
> (Mic 6:8).

These words from the prophet Micah are one of the most "quotable quotes" of the Old Testament. They have been the subject of annual sermons and the saying displayed on innumerable banners; they entered the political arena when they were quoted by President Carter in his inaugural address in January, 1977. The phrase "to do justice" is cited by the American Bishops in their Pastoral Letter on the Economy as the epitome of the message of the prophets, "the substance of prophetic faith."[1]

The imperative for social justice found its classic expression among the eighth century prophets, Amos, Micah and Isaiah.[2]

---

[1] *Economic Justice for All: Catholic Social Teaching and the U.S. Economy,* (USCCB, 1986) #37

[2] For a very insightful interpretation of the eighth century prophets organized around the three demands of Mic 6:8 "What the Lord Requires: Justice, Covenant Loyalty, The Humble Walk," see Bernhard W. Anderson, *The Eighth Century Prophets: Amos, Hosea, Isaiah, Micah,* Proclamation Commentaries, (Fortress, 1978).

Amos, for instance, addressed a society of great wealth, at a time of unprecedented economic prosperity. The archaeological findings from recent digs at Tirzah (Tell el Far'a, once capital of the northern kingdom) confirm this in that they visibly display the great disparity between the spacious, expensively constructed houses of the wealthy and the tiny homes of the poor in a separate part of the city. Amos pronounced doom upon "those who lie upon beds of ivory and stretch themselves upon their couches" (6:4), while they "oppress the poor" and "crush the needy" (4:1). Theirs was a wealth accumulated at the expense of the poor whom "they sell for silver" (2:6), in direct violation of specific Mosaic laws intended to safeguard the rights of the needy (compare 2:8 "they lay themselves down beside every altar upon garments taken in pledge" with Deut 24:12-13 "and if he is a poor man, you shall not sleep in his pledge; when the sun goes down, you shall restore to him the pledge that he may sleep in his cloak and bless you"). Other prophets took up the technical language of the courts, and described God as entering into a lawsuit with the people. "The Lord has taken his place to contend [to conduct a legal case]" (Isa 3:14); the charge: "it is you who have devoured the vineyard, the spoil of the poor is in your houses. What do you mean by crushing my people, by grinding the face of the poor, says the Lord God of hosts" (Isa 3:14-15).

For these prophets, justice is a theological term, not just a matter of philosophical debate or abstract speculation. It is rooted in the knowledge of Israel's God, a God who is just and requires justice. This justice involves the fulfilling of responsibilities in relationships (between ruler and people, citizen and alien, priest and congregation). The prophets focused upon certain clearly defined issues: control of the land (not as a neutral commodity to be bought and sold as the market dictates, but as an inheritance from the Lord to *all* the people—Isa 5:8-10); the juridical sphere (justice for the poor in the courts—no bribes, Isa 1:21-22); accumulation of wealth in the hands of a few. In all these areas, the ultimate test, the litmus case for true justice is the treatment of widows and orphans, those in society who, more than any other, are most vulnerable, with no one to guarantee their rights. In the words of Rabbi Heschel, "Prophecy is the voice that God has lent to the silent agony, a voice to the plundered poor, to the profaned riches of the world." [3] Thus, justice is not a utopian dream to be achieved in some far distant time-to-come; it must be expressed now in the concrete social, economic, and political decisions of the society.

For the prophet Jeremiah, it is the very exercise of such justice which defines what it means to *know God*. As the monarchy drew to a close, Jeremiah made one last attempt to call the king to his rightful duty as guarantor of justice. Since the days of the Babylonian king Hammurabi (1800 BC) the ideology of ancient Near Eastern monarchy had challenged the king to rule so that "the strong may not oppress the weak, that justice be dealt to orphans and widows." The "job description" of the Davidic monarch was even more precise:

> He delivers the needy when he calls,
> the poor and him who has no helper.
> He has pity on the weak and the needy,
> and saves the lives of the needy.
> From oppression and violence he redeems their life;
> and precious is their blood in his sight.
>
> (Ps 72:12-14)

[3] Abraham Heschel, *The Prophets: An Introduction*, (Harper & Row, 1962), p. 5.

But Jeremiah castigates King Jehoiakim for succumbing to the illusion that it is a luxurious palace which makes the king, a mansion literally built at human expense, "Woe to him who builds his house by unrighteousness, and his upper rooms by injustice; who makes his neighbor serve him for nothing, and does not give him his wages" (Jer 22:13). In contrast, Jehoiakim's father Josiah "who walked in all the way of David his father" (II Kgs 22:2) knew what it was to "do justice and righteousness" (Jer 22:15):

> He judged the cause of the poor and needy;
> then it was well.
> Is not this to know me?
> says the Lord.
>
> (22:16)

For Jeremiah, to know God is not a matter of intellectual assent to religious truths, nor even the performance of religious duties. The Mexican biblical scholar José Miranda states the case in absolute starkness: "Yahweh is known only in the human act of achieving justice and compassion for the neighbor."[4]

Justice And Cult

What then is the relationship between the prophetic world of justice and the priestly domain of cult and religious observance, of Temple, sacrifice and ritual purity? We have already noted that priest and prophet seem to come together in the

---

[4]José Miranda, *Marx and the Bible: A Critique of the Philosophy of Oppression*, (Orbis, 1974) p. 49.

post-exilic period. Was this an attempted fusion of two irreconcilable opposites? As prophets became more priestly, did they maintain their passion for justice? Or, was it lost, submerged in more mundane concerns, smothered by the minutiae which seem part and parcel of cultic life? As will be demonstrated repeatedly in the following pages, the issues are critical to our understanding of the spirituality of the post-exilic prophets.

Even the questions which we ask here are shaped by the concerns we bring to the enterprise. Our posing of the issue in precisely this way in itself a reflection of one of the primary areas of tension in modern spirituality: the relationship between liturgy and justice. In the years since the Second Vatican Council we have seen two radical developments, one in the area of liturgical change and renewal (use of the vernacular, development of new rites and reform of older ones, expanded ministries for the laity, etc.), and the second in a heightened concern for justice, the awareness that "actions on behalf of justice and participation in the transformation of the world appear to us a constitutive dimension of the preaching of the gospel."[5] Yet, it often seems as if these two movements pass by each other like ships in the night. The social activists scorn those concerned with "smells and bells"; the liturgists look down on those who are only concerned with "doing."

Fundamental to all our discussion is the enduring insight of the eighth century prophets: cult can never be a substitute for the lived reality of justice in the social-political-economic sphere. Amos thunders:

> I hate, I despise your feasts,
> and I take no delight in your solemn assemblies.

[5]*Justice in the World*, 1971 Synod of Bishops, (USCCB, 1972), p. 34.

> Even though you offer me your burnt offerings and cereal
> offerings,
> I will not accept them,
> and the peace offerings of your fatted beasts,
> I will not look upon.
> Take away from me the noise of your songs;
> to the melody of your harps I will not listen.
> But let justice roll down like waters,
> and righeousness like an ever-flowing stream.
>
> (5:21-24)

It was on the basis of such passages that, in the last century, there was often an attempt to portray the prophets as advocates of "pure spiritual religion" freed from all cult and ritual, all such "popish" additions. Now scholars recognize that such a view is far too neat, influenced more by the presuppositions of nineteenth century rationalism than by the prophetic world-view. Amos was not against cult; he was against any claim that mere cultic observance could substitute for the demands of justice. To stand with Amos requires that we affirm, as our starting point, that worship is an expression of, not a substitute for, social responsibility.

The Demands of Justice and Cult in Ezekiel

When we come to Ezekiel, we see for the first time the combination of a prophetic and priestly calling. Ezekiel is clearly a priest, operating within the contours of priestly theology; the Temple, cult and purity are important and indispensable realities. Thus, Ezekiel insists that disaster came "because you have defiled my sanctuary with all your detestable things and with all your abominations, therefore I will cut you down" (5:11). When the hand of God lifts the prophet to "a very high mountain" (40:2) for a vision of the world which is to come, it is a vision centered on the Temple, "the place of my throne . . . where I will dwell in the midst of the people of Israel forever" (43:7). Even the additions—which we find so absolutely boring—of innumerable regulations for the conduct of sacrifice, the duties of the Levites and Zadokite priests, the parceling out of the land, all this is not just the indulgence of mere pedantry, but the concrete enfleshment of a vision—a priestly vision. Given this intense concern for the cult, what has happened to the prophetic passion for justice?

One answer can be derived from an examination of chapter 18. This is a chapter which is frequently quoted as an illustration of the increasing emphasis on personal responsibility which marked this period of religious thought. The discusssion takes the form of a disputation between Ezekiel and the people. Quoting an ancient proverb, "The fathers have eaten sour grapes and the children's teeth are set on edge" (18:2), the people complain that they are suffering unjustly for the sins of their ancestors. Given that God is "a jealous God, visiting the iniquity of the fathers upon the children to the third and fourth generation" (Ex. 20:5, an ancient formulaic text), the scene is set for the people to deny their own sinfulness; to quote from Lamentations, "Our fathers sinned and are no more; and we bear their iniquities" (5:7). Throughout chapter 18, at great length, Ezekiel develops the contrary argument until he can draw the conclusion "the soul that sins shall die. The son shall not suffer for the iniquity of the father, nor the father suffer for the iniquity of the son" (18:20).

What is of particular interest to us here is not, however, the arguments for individual responsibility, but the way in which Ezekiel describes the righteous person (18:5-9), the wicked person (18:10-13), and the righteous child of a wicked father (18:14-18). When Ezekiel undertakes to describe the righteous person, what does he include: is it the cultic requirements that we expect from a priest, or does he look to the prophetic concern for justice expressed in action? The fullest description of a person who "is righteous and does what is lawful and right" comes in verses 5-9. (The fact that Ezekiel is probably not formulating these lists *de nouveau*, but drawing upon traditional material, whether a priestly Torah (Ps 15, 24:3-6) or wisdom material (Job 31), is not at issue here; what is important is *what* he chooses to include from tradition). Ezekiel gives twelve points in his description of the righteous person. Reading the list, we quickly realize that we are in a very different world from that of Amos. The righteous

> does not eat upon the mountains
> or lift up his eyes to the idols of the house of Israel,
> does not defile his neighbor's wife
> or approach a woman in her time of impurity
>
> (18:6)

Clearly this is the world of the priest, the world in which matters of cultic purity, and laws of sexual pollution are of major importance. However, reading further along, we could well be hearing Amos speaking: the righteous person

> does not oppress any one,
> but restores to the debtor his pledge,
> commits no robbery,
> gives his bread to the hungry
> and covers the naked with a garment,
> goes not lend at interest or take any increase,
> withholds his hand from iniquity. . . .
>
> (18:7-8).

Thus, in a style reminiscent of the Decalogue, the cultic concerns are listed first, followed by the demands in the socio-economic order; this second list is twice as long and culminates with the positive demand to execute "true justice between people" (18:8). For Ezekiel, obedience to both cultic law and fulfillment of the demands of justice are essential to the profile of the righteous. The introduction of the cultic-legal prescriptions is a new emphasis for prophecy, but it does not negate or replace the uncompromising demand to act with justice.

The Post-Exilic Prophets

In so much of the current discussion of justice—in sermons, parish discussion groups, social justice educational material, popular spiritual books—virtually no mention is made of the post-exilic prophets. It is Amos, Micah, Isaiah and Jeremiah who are presented as *the* prophets of justice. Where are the later prophets? It is undeniable that passionate calls for the exercise of social justice are much less common in later prophets; there are simply fewer "quotable quotes" on justice. But rather than assuming that this necessarily attests to a deficiency in prophecy at this stage, perhaps we need to rethink some of our fundamental premises concerning the work and concerns of the prophet.

There is a danger today in making *one* theme or *one* concern the sole focus of both our interest in and our evaluation of the prophets. Even among the eighth century prophets whom we examined earlier, social justice does not exhaust the agenda of the prophetic vocation. The persistent attack on apostasy and idolatry is also central to their concerns, although perhaps not as immediately applicable to our situation nor as palatable to our sensibilities. Most of the prophetic books devote a major section of the total material to oracles against the foreign nations (eg. Isa 12-23, Jer 46-51, Ezek 25-32)—we scarcely know what to do with that material today. Similarly, attention to the rebuilding of the Temple, this vision of a restored community which is given expression in details of temple measurement, priestly functions and orders, concern with ritual purity—all this seems to us so institutionalized, so pragmatic. We want to say "so unprophetic," but that is because we have, whether consciously or not, accepted a certain definition of what is prophetic. The later prophets serve to remind us that we risk confining and restricting the message of prophecy, both in its time and in ours, if we persist in reading and judging only through the lens of a specific theme of our own choosing—even so important a theme as social justice.

Furthermore, if we take seriously that the prophets spoke to concrete situations and real needs in actual social-political-economic situations, the radical differences between the world of the eighth century BC and the world of the fifth-fourth centuries BC require that the approach to justice will be different. To recall our earlier discussion, the eighth century was a time of bitter socio-economic change and conflict; Judah was an independent state, with a quickly widening gap between the rich and poor. The loss of political independence and the subsequent loss of economic control, the shift of power from a centralized king and court to a foreign power governing from Samaria, the increasing involvement of the leading priestly families both politically and economically—all this must have affected the socio-economic life in ways which cannot be totally documented from the surviving evidence. At least in the years immediately following the return, the community probably did not face blatant economic disparity among its members; everyone shared the very real poverty and economic struggles in this "day of small things" (Zech 4:10).

Furthermore, our ability to "read" the justice concerns of the prophets is, in a sense, dependent upon the particular form which their words took. In the oracles of judgement of the pre-exilic prophets, the very form of speech called for a detailed exposition of the reasons for the divine word of judgement. Literally dozens of oracles attest to a standard format: summons to the addressee; enumeration of the specific reasons for judgement; the announcement of judgement ("therefore" . . .). The very shape of the oracle provides the space to outline, as it were, the economic abuses and oppressions, often at considerable length and in graphic detail. But, at the time of Exile, as the standard forms of prophetic speech changed, we find new genres: promises of salvation, proclamations of salvation, disputations, visions. The standard format of the promise of salvation, for instance, includes address, assurance of salvation, basis of salvation, consequence of God's action—but there is no place structually to discuss justice concerns per se. In point of fact, however, many of the oracles of salvation do portray a vision of justice, plenty and prosperity for all. Note, for example, Joel 3:18:

> And in that day, the mountains shall drip sweet wine,
> and the hills shall flow with milk,
> and all the stream beds of Judah shall flow with water,
> and a fountain shall come forth from the house of the Lord.

The salvation promised includes an abundance of food and water for all—this is the reality of *shalom*, a reversal of poverty and want. The justice concern is not so explicit nor readily apparent to us today because of our tendency to read the salvation oracles in a very spiritualized sense.

I have indicated that the issue of social justice is not the *only* concern of the later prophets, and that their "value" (to put that word into quotation marks) as prophets is not to be judged solely in terms of explicit attention to this particular theme. Still, as the following examples will illustrate, in a new political and economic situation, when the very forms of prophetic speech had changed radically and when prophecy itself was becoming more priestly and more apocalyptic, the later prophets did continue to uphold justice as an integral and essential element in what is meant for the community to know its God.

Isaiah 58:1-14: "Is Not This The Fast?"

Is not this the fast that I choose:
to loose the bonds of wickedness,
to undo the thongs of the yoke,
to let the oppressed go free,
and to break every yoke?
Is it not to share your bread with the hungry,
and bring the homeless poor into your house;
when you see the naked to cover him,
and not to hide yourself from your own flesh?
(58:6-7)

Let us begin with the combination of the themes of justice and fasting in Isaiah 58, a lengthy text with hints of complex development. Clearly the issue of fasting was of particular concern for the post-exilic community (we shall see this again in our discussion of Zech 7-8, pp. 134-136). In the pre-exilic period, fasting had been primarily an expression of mourning (1 Sam 31:13, 2 Sam 1:12, 3:35), or a response to a crisis (Josh 7:6, Judg 20:26, 1 Sam 7:6). By weeping, the tearing of one's clothes, putting on sackcloth and ashes, and other ritual activities, the person fasting sought to arouse the pity and compassion of God. At the time of the destruction in 587 BC, we know that a series of public communal fasts were initiated to mourn the events connected with the catastrophe (a fast in the fifth month to commemorate the burning of the city, in the seventh month for the murder of Gedaliah, in the fourth and the tenth months commemorating the initial breach in the walls and the beginning of exile; see Zech 7:3, 8:19).

Our passage begins with the summons, "Cry aloud, spare not, lift up your voice like a trumpet; declare to my people their transgression, to the house of Jacob their sins" (58:1). In the style typical of the later prophets, Third Isaiah draws upon earlier standard prophetic language (e.g. Hos 8:1, "Set the trumpet to your lips"; Mic 3:8, "to declare to Jacob his transgression and to Israel his sin)." The people ask "Why have we fasted and you do not see us?" (58:3). The Lord replies with words of indictment: they pursue their own business on a fast day; they oppress their workers; they quarrel and fight. They are meticulous about the external observances, the bowing down and the sackcloth and ashes, but these alone will not attract divine attention; the mere observance of rituals of fasting is not an automatic guarantee that God will respond. In the key verses quoted above (58:6-7), the Lord goes on to spell out the nature of a true fast: to loose the bonds of wickedness, to undo the thongs of the yoke, to free the oppressed, to break every yoke, to share bread with the hungry, to house the homeless, and cover the naked. For a people who had themselves recently experienced delivery from slavery and exile, the language is especially poignant, "to loose . . . to undo . . . to let the oppressed go free . . . to break the yoke." The true fast is not a negative doing without, but a positive doing for: to share bread with the hungry, bring the homeless into your own houses, clothe the naked. Only when this is being done, can there be the expectation of salvation, "Then shall your light break forth like the dawn and your healing shall spring up speedily" (58:8).

The prophet acknowledges that the magnificent salvation promised by Second Isaiah is not yet a reality in the struggling community. His message is fundamentally the same as the eighth century prophets: the problem lies not in the realm of cultic observance, but in the realm of relationships between people. Without a just society, one in which the poor are fed, the naked clothed, the homeless housed, salvation cannot come to pass. The eighth century prophets had pointed out the danger of cult becoming a false idol—something which promises a salvation which it cannot give. Now when fasting had acquired a central place in the worship life of the post-exilic community, the voice of prophecy tackles this new form of cultic observance which likewise has the potential for becoming a substitute for real acts of justice.

Zechariah 5: A Scroll And An Ephah

For a further examination of how the post-exilic prophets dealt with justice concerns, let us turn next to Zechariah 5, a chapter which is likely to be much less familiar to most of us. Zechariah is not a prophet whom one readily connects with this issue at all! He was probably a priest himself and identified

in many ways with the traditional priestly worldview. In a
series of seven visions, dated precisely to Feb. 519 BC,
Zechariah described, in highly symbolic form, his ideal for the
restored community—with the Temple at the center (the
menorah of the central vision—chapter 4), governed by
Zerubbabel and Joshua the high priest (the two olive
trees—4:3).

As in all priestly theology, Zechariah has a keen sense of the
question: how can a transcendent and holy God dwell among
a sinful people? In taking up this question in chapter five,
Zechariah uses neither the standard form of a judgement
oracle in the manner of the pre-exilic prophets, nor the
sermonic-hortatory mode of chapters 7-8. Rather, the genre is
this one of vision—a symbolic representation which, in terms
of development and complexity of form, is midway between
the short and straightforward visions of Amos (e.g., the basket
of summer fruit 8:1-2) and the lengthy, elaborate apocalyptic
visions of Daniel (e.g., the magnificent vision of the four beasts
rising from the sea in chapter 7). Thus, when Zechariah
expresses justice concerns they are both revealed and concealed
in the language of imagery and symbol. It is not for naught that
St. Jerome called this *obscurissimus liber*!

Zechariah 5:1-4: The Vision of the Scroll

Again I lifted my eyes and saw, and behold, a flying scroll!
And he said to me, "What do you see?" I answered, "I see a
flying scroll; its length is twenty cubits, and its breadth ten
cubits." Then he said to me, "This is the curse which goes out
over the face of the whole land; for every one who steals shall be
cut off henceforth according to it, and every one who swears
falsely shall be cut off henceforth according to it. I will send
it forth, says the Lord of hosts, and it shall enter the house of

the thief, and the house of him who swears falsely by my name; and it shall abide in his house and consume it, both timber and stones.

The prophet lifts up his eyes and sees—a flying scroll. After Zechariah boldly identifies what he sees, the angel queries him again as if to say "Now really, let's get this right—what *do* you see?" The prophet insists—a flying scroll of monstrous proportions: 20 cubits by 10 cubits (precisely the dimensions of the porch of Solomon's temple (1 Kgs 6:3). The angel then identifies the scroll as "the curse that goes out" to everyone who steals and swears falsely. The Hebrew text here is difficult and can be read in different ways (compare "for everyone who steals will be cut off henceforth according to it" or "everyone who steals have remained up till now unpunished"). The vision ends with the angel explaining that the curse will consume the house of the thief and the one who swears falsely.

Although some of the precise details of the vision are puzzling, the general thrust is clear: the removal of sin is a prerequisite to divine presence. Sin is removed, not by any human agency or effort, but by the power of God. The curse here is an object of awe and terror—an active and real power to bring about destruction and death; like the word of God (Isa 55:11), it is efficacious, capable of accomplishing that for which it is sent. In the Old Testament, the curse is invoked when the perpetrator of a crime is unknown (e.g. Judg 17:2 where an Ephraimite women utters a curse against the unknown thief who has stolen one thousand pieces of silver), or when a accusation cannot be proven (e.g. the woman accused of adultery in Num 5:21-28). In addition, the covenant between the Lord and the people included a lengthy and detailed list of "all the curses of the covenant" (Deut 29:21) to come upon those who violate covenant stipulations (Deut 28:15-68).

In this vision, the particular concerns are the thief and the one who swears falsely. Why the concern with these two crimes? Although at the time of exile complaints were voiced about expropriation of the land (Ezek 33:24), there is less evidence that land theft was an issue for Zechariah. The precise naming of the second group ("the ones that swear falsely by my name" 5:4) is unusual (the phrase is found only in Lev 19:12 which may be later than our text). It is really a combination of Ex 20:7, the command of the Decalogue about taking the name of the Lord in vain, and Ex 20:16, the commandment about swearing falsely against one's neighbor. The language is clearly meant to recall the Decalogue. Through the symbolic representation of this awesome flying scroll, Zechariah indicates that, in the restored community, those who violate either the commandments concerned with God (typified by swearing falsely) or the commandments concerned with neighbor (typified by the thief) will be punished by the curse. In this new community, even when the king has disappeared and the forms of governance are radically altered, the old ethos of the Decalogue is still normative.

Zechariah 5:5-11: *The Ephah and the Woman*

> Then the angel who talked with me came forward and
> said to me, "Lift your eyes and see what this is that
> goes forth." And I said, "What is it?" He said, "This is the ephah
> that goes forth." And he said, "This is their iniquity in all the
> land." And behold, the leaden cover was lifted, and there was a
> woman sitting in the ephah! And he said, "This is Wickedness."
> And he thrust her back into the ephah, and thrust down the
> leaden weight upon its mouth.
> Then I lifted my eyes and saw, and behold, two women coming

forward! The wind was in their wings; they had wings like the wings of a stork, and they lifted up the ephah between earth and heaven. Then I said to the angel who talked with me. "Where are they taking the ephah?" He said to me, "To the land of Shinar, to build a house for it; and when this is prepared, they will set the ephah down there on its base.

This is a vision even more puzzling than the previous one. Now the prophet looks and doesn't seem willing to venture an opinion on what he sees (perhaps after his previous experience, he figures it is better to keep silent!); instead he asks, "What is it?" The angel explains that this is an ephah, a dry measuring basket of some five to nine gallons, which like the scroll in the previous vision is in motion. He further explains "This is their iniquity in all the land." (Our translation follows the Greek and Syriac text here; the Hebrew reads "This is their eye [i.e. what they see] in all the land"). Then the cover is lifted from the ephah to reveal a woman who is identified with wickedness. She is pushed back into the ephah and two other women appear with the wind in their wings to carry the ephah off to Shinar (Babylon) where a house (temple) is to be built for it.

All commentators readily admit that this is the most bizzare and difficult of the visions—I have no illusions that I can explain it totally here. A common interpretation would run something like this: "Where as the sixth vision spoke of cleansing the community from all sin, the seventh speaks of the removal of all false and idolatrous worship." In this rendering, wickedness is interpreted specifically as idolatry which is carried off to the land of idolatry. However, as Margaret Baker pointed out a few years ago,[6] there is another, and ancient, tradition of interpretation, an approach which

[6]Margaret Baker, "Economic Ills in Zechariah," *Heythrop Journal*, 19, 1978, pp. 20-26.

sees the issue at stake not as idolatry, but as economic abuses. The Targum (the Aramaic translation) comments, "These are the people who were giving and receiving with false measures." While there is little evidence that idolatry was an issue of vital concern for Zechariah's community in 520 BC, certainly this was a time of economic instability in which conditions were ripe for exploitation and cheating as money poured in from Babylon for rebuilding projects. A number of small but intriguing points in this passage (which we cannot examine in any detail here) support the interpretation which sees economic abuses at stake. In the prophets, the ephah so often comes up in discussions of just/unjust weight (Deut 25:14, 15; Amos 8:5, Prov 20:10, Lev 19:36, Ezek 45:10, Micah 6:11) that the mention of term would invoke the economic sphere. The mysterious "two women coming forward" (reading according to the standard Hebrew) could be "two moneylenders" (if the Hebrew is pointed slightly differently, as in Neh 5:10, 11). There is reason then to suggest—although it can only be a suggestion—that, in this vision, Zechariah may again be concerned specifically with the removal of economic abuses and exploitation within the community, a removal which is prerequisite for the divine presence.

Zechariah 7-8

The concern with the concrete socio-economic life of the community and the removal of abuses and exploitation as a prerequisite for the inauguration of the new age finds expression not only in the language of vision, but also in the oracles and sermon in Zechariah 7-8. Once again, we are dealing with two very complex chapters and it is possible only to focus on a few points relevant to our concerns. Certainly these chapters have undergone extensive editorial activity and ordering; in the final form of the text as we have it; material which was probably quite diverse in origin and genre, is now brought together and dated to Dec. 7, 518 BC (7:1).

Certain people (the text here can be read in a number of different ways; it is not totally clear who they are, or where they have come from or to) arrive to ask the priests and the prophets, "Should I mourn and fast in the fifth month as I have done for so many years?" As we saw in our study of Isaiah 58, the issue of fasting was a real one within the life of the Restoration community and involved a fourfold series of commemorative fasts throughout the year (see p. 128). Were these fasts to be maintained now that the Exile was over and the community in the process of being rebuilt? The prophet does not offer an answer to the question until the closing verses of chapter 8 when it comes in the form of an oracle from the Lord: these fasts shall be "to the house of Judah seasons of joy and gladness, and cheerful feasts" (Zech 8:19). A new age is dawning, an age of blessing which will find expression in feasts, not fasts. But the oracle concludes with an admonition, "Love truth and peace," that is, "Love those things which make for a full and faithful life."[7] The new age does not negate, in fact it demands, the doing of truth and peace.

The large section between the question in 7:3 and the answer in 8:18 is material from diverse sources which has been drawn only secondarily into the framework of the fasting question. Picking up on a theme established in the very beginning of the book (1:2-6), Zechariah reiterates that the

[7]This is the translation of Peter Ackroyd, *Exile and Restoration*, (SCM Press, 1968), p. 209.

past has continuing relevance for the present; the message of "the former prophets" (1:4, 7:7) is still applicable. This is especially clear in 7:8-10 where the ethical concerns of the earlier prophets are placed in the imperative for the community, "render true judgement, show kindness and mercy, do not oppress the widow, the fatherless, the sojourner, or the poor; and let none of you devise evil against his brother in your heart." The list is both traditional (compare Jer 22:3) and innovative; the specific addition of "the poor" to the standard prophetic concern for the widow, fatherless and sojourner perhaps reflects conditions in the community.

In chapter 8, we have a series of oracles of salvation dealing with the blessing to come. The God who once determined to judge in anger now determines to "do good to Jerusalem and to the house of Judah" (8:14-15). The language is richly covenantal ("they shall be my people and I will be their God, in faithfulness and righteousness'—8:8) but is followed by imperatives, "Speak the truth to one another; render in your gates judgements that are true and make for peace, do not devise evil in your hearts . . . (8:16-17). Zechariah's picture of *shalom* is a subdued one, expressed in the language of realism: "Old men and old women shall again sit in the streets of Jerusalem, each with staff in hand for very age. And the streets of the city shall be full of boys and girls playing in its streets" (8:4-5). This is not yet the full-blown apocalyptic language of "new heavens and a new earth" where the wolf and the lamb lie down together (Isa 65:17-25, see pp. 153-154). In this vision, truth is still something to be done; peace is something to be pursued. For Zechariah, this ethical imperative is an integral component of the new age.

Isaiah 61

The Spirit of the Lord God is upon me,
because the Lord has anointed me
to bring good tidings to the afflicted,
he has sent me to bind up the brokenhearted,
to proclaim liberty to the captives
and the opening of the prison to those who are bound;
to proclaim the year of the Lord's favor
and the day of vengeance of our God;
to comfort all who mourn.

(61:1-2)

For our final example, we turn to what is probably the most well-known passage in all the later prophetic corpus. According to Luke's gospel, these were the words chosen by Jesus to inaugurate his public ministry and proclaim the kingdom:

> He went to the synagogue, as his custom was, on the Sabbath day. And he stood up to read; and there was given to him the book of the prophet Isaiah. He opened the book and found the place where it was written,
> The Spirit of the Lord is upon me . . . "

(Lk 4:16-18)

In Luke's gospel, the text Jesus reads is not an exact rendering of Isaiah 61 (even as found in the Greek Septuagint); the phrase about binding up the broken-hearted is omitted, and the line "to set at liberty those who are oppressed" is inserted from Isa 58:6, suggesting that Luke too saw a close connection between these two passages from Isaiah.

The opening verse of Isaiah 61 echoes the beginning of the first Servant Song, "Behold, my servant, whom I uphold, my chosen in whom my soul delights; I have put my Spirit upon him," (Isa 42:1). Our text in Isaiah 61 is sometimes called the

Fifth Servant Song, even though the specific term "servant" is never used (we will be discussing the Servant Songs in the final chapter, see pp. 178-182). As with all the Servant Songs, the question is whether the prophet is referring to an individual or a group—is the subject of the poem the prophet himself describing his vocation, or is it the community, or is it perhaps some specific group within the community? The ambiguity may be intentional; the mission of the prophet and the mission of the community are indelibly fused.

The speaker has been anointed, a term both prophetic and royal, and has been given a mission "to bring good tidings to the afflicted." The Hebrew word here *(anawin)* is multivalent; "the afflicted" are those who are materially poor and those who are utterly dependent on God. The anointed of the Lord is "to bring *good news*"; the image is that of a military runner who brings news of the victory in battle (1 Sam 31:9; 2 Sam 18:19-21). Again the prophet is drawing from Second Isaiah for whom the same term "good news" (40:9; 41:27; 52:7) applied to the imminent deliverance of the people from exile. Now the people have returned as Second Isaiah announced, but the prophet is again to bring good tidings of things yet to be accomplished; in this sense, the passage is profoundly eschatological.

The prophet is very specific about what this good news will encompass: "to bind up the broken-hearted, to proclaim liberty to the captives, and the opening of the prison to those who are bound." All of these are released from some condition of enslavement; thus the culmination of the Servant's mission is "to proclaim liberty to the captives . . . to proclaim the year of the Lord's favor and the day of vengeance of our God" (61:2). These are technical terms from the description of the Jubilee year in Lev 25: "You shall hallow the fiftieth year and proclaim liberty throughout the land to all its inhabitants; it shall be a jubilee for you, when each of you shall return to his property and each of you shall return to his family" (Lev 25:10). Although many details about the Jubilee Year are uncertain (whether it was ever actually held, the precise legislation governing how to count the years and how to execute the concrete prescriptions[8]), we know the basic concept which the year sought to embody: every fiftieth year was to be a year of release from conditions which enslave. Israelites who had been forced to sell their ancestral land were to have it restored; Israelites who had been forced to sell themselves into slavery would be released; the land would lie fallow. As part of the Holiness code with its emphasis on cultic purity, these Jubilee laws bear witness to a profound understanding of God as sovereign: the land and the people belong to God. But this has serious ethical implications: if God is sovereign, those who are trapped in slavery and indebtedness for a time are assured of an ultimate day of release. Therefore, when the prophet seeks to announce the age to come it is in terms of the Jubilee year. Salvation will mean release and deliverance precisely for the poor, for those in prison, for those who mourn and are broken-hearted. The image of the Jubilee is continued on in the next verse in the language of the "year of the Lord's favor" and the "day of vengeance." Whereas, for the pre-exilic prophets, the Day of the Lord was a day of judgement (e.g. Amos 5:18-20, Zeph 1:14-16; with these later prophets the judgement element has faded entirely; the day of God's

[8]For a more detailed discussion of the Jubilee Year, see Robert Gnuse, "Jubilee Legislation in Leviticus: Israel's Vision of Social Reform" *Biblical Theology Bulletin*, April 1985, pp. 43-48. For the theological implications of Jubilee, see Sharon Ringe, *Jesus, Liberation and the Biblical Jubilee: Images for Ethics and Christology* , Overtures to Biblical Theology 19, (Fortress, 1985), especially pp. 91-97.

vengeance has a totally salvific thrust (compare Isa 35:4).

By adopting specific Jubilee language in his vision of the eschatological salvation, Third Isaiah prevents us from taking the magnificent promises solely in a "spiritualized" sense. When God's reign, as announced by the prophet, breaks into human history, it will find its realization in the political, economic and social spheres of life. On the one hand, we can and rightly must read Isaiah's list of those who are to be the recipients of divine favor in the widest and most inclusive sense; that is, the captives, the afflicted, the prisoners, those who mourn, encompass all those who suffer, all those who await deliverance in any aspect of their life. But this expansive vision is rooted concretely in the Jubilee reality of those who experience actual release and deliverance from debt, from physical enslavement, and from loss of their ancestral land. This Jubilee proclamation of a new age of release and freedom is a dramatic expression of the abiding prophetic conviction that the reign of God is always to be found in the doing of justice (Mic 6:8).

6

A FUTURE AND A HOPE

For I know the plans I have for you, says the Lord, . . . to give you a future and a hope

(Jer 29:11)

Within the post-exilic prophetic corpus, there is a particular and distinctive group of texts—texts which are beautiful and inspiring at the same time that they are elusive and frustrating and in some ways frightening. It is often tempting simply to forget about such passages and to focus our attention on those texts which seem more relevant to our immediate situation and concerns. Yet this cluster of passages—Isa 65-66, Zech 9-14, Joel 2:28-3:21, Ezek 38-39, Isa 24-27, Mal 4 (the list is meant to be descriptive rather than exhaustive)—is a substantial and integral part of post-exilic prophecy. These texts are by no means expressive of a peripheral interest or the concern of a few maverick individuals.

All of these texts deal in some way with a vision of the future; not the future as tomorrow or the next day, but a more distant future "on that day." This is a future which is largely outside the realm of world history; for instance, the enemy which is to be defeated is not a single neighboring empire, but "the nations" or even "Leviathan the fleeing serpent . . . the dragon that is in the sea " (Isa 27:1). In this type of prophecy there is a notable absence of the historical specificity which undergirded Second Isaiah's concern with an immediate future in which a concrete Persian king (Cyrus) and a physical geographical movement (from Babylon to Judah) would be the pivotal foci. In the later prophets, even texts which seem to be rooted very concretely (for example, Zech 9:1-17 with its lists of places Hadrach, Damascus, Philistia, etc.) are not necessarily to be read in terms of "real" geography.[1] Yet, paradoxically, the vision of the future is still "this-worldly." It does not look for answers in some sort of other-wordly existence, nor in terms of a purely individual salvation; rather, these prophets are passionately convinced that God will intervene to transform *this* world, in ways and at a time still only faintly glimpsed.

The specific collection of prophetic texts which we are examining in this chapter is of increasing interest today as we are beginning to discover for ourselves that a living and dynamic thrust toward the future is an integral element of a true Christian spirituality, that in living the Christian life *hope* is just as essential a virtue as faith and charity. In much of traditional theology, concern for eschatology was reduced to a "harmless little chapter at the end of dogmatic theology"[2] and, in the practical order, to a series of sermons on "the four last things"—death, judgement, heaven, hell—preached at the

---

[1]See the discussion of Zechariah 9 by Paul Hanson, *The Dawn of Apocalyptic: The Historical and Social Roots of Jewish Apocalyptic Eschatology*, (Fortress, 1975), pp 292-324.

[2]Karl Barth, *Der Romerbrief*, (Munich, 1922), p 486; quoted by Zachary Hayes, *What Are They Saying About the End of the World?* (Paulist, 1983). This little book can serve as a good introduction to the way in which the traditional questions of eschatology are being examined anew.

annual parish mission. Though it may be somewhat of an overstatement to claim (as some have) that "all theology begins and ends with eschatology," it has become increasingly clear that those parts of the prophetic corpus which speak of the future must be taken with absolute seriousness in our reflection on the totality of the biblical message.

A bewildering variety of terms have been used to describe these texts—"eschatological," "apocalyptic," "proto-apocalyptic," "prophetic eschatology," apocalyptic eschatology" and more. This type of careful attention to terminology, exact classification of differing materials, and concern for typological development belongs to the realm of the scholar, and has, in fact, proven to be most helpful in ordering and understanding what otherwise would be an undifferentiated mass of texts. But for our purposes here, we do not need to get bogged down in what to call these texts, as long as we recognize that different scholars will use different terminology even for the same text.

Eschatology, in and of itself, is a tricky term. Certain scholars will readily speak of the eschatology of the eighth century prophets, while others will be hesitant to use the term even with regard to the thought of the fifth century prophets. Certainly if we define eschatology in the strict sense of "last things" (from the Greek *eschata*)—that is, the stopping point where the world, history and time end—there is little eschatology even in the latest prophets. Such full-blown dualistic speculation only comes in certain later Jewish books, in passages such as 4 Ezra 7:30-31 (from the end of the first century AD):

> And the world shall be turned back to primeval
> silence for seven days, as it was at the first

> beginning, so that no one shall be left. And after
> seven days the world, which is not awake, shall be
> roused, and that which is corruptible shall perish.

However, it is also possible to speak of eschatology in a more limited sense. The pre-exilic prophets did speak with a sense of future expectation in the announcements such as "the end has come upon my people Israel" (Amos 8:2). Amos, for instance, described this time of dramatic divine intervention in the terminology of "the Day of the Lord" which was familiar to his audience—but he turned the concept completely around. For Amos, the Day of the Lord would be a time, not of salvation as the people so self-confidently and automatically assumed, but of judgement, a day of "darkness, and not light, and gloom with no brightness in it" (Amos 5:20)—the day on which the kingdom of Israel would experience the full on-slaught of the Assyrian armies.

The later prophets continued to develop this eschatological thrust. The anonymous prophets Third Isaiah, Deutero-Zechariah, and the author of Isaiah 24-27 refused to believe that either the present political reality (the might of the Persian Empire) or the specific shape of the restored community (with the Zadokite priesthood in control) were the final fulfillment of God's promises. In these prophets, the focus shifts more and more to the *future* as the arena of God's action. The focus is on what *God* can and will do, with surprisingly little emphasis on human agents or human responsibility.

This is perhaps one of the reasons why, in the twentieth century with our very personal and individualistic orientation, we find these texts so foreign to our thinking. With more or less unconscious self-centeredness, we assume that every bib-lical text should tell us what *we* should do, and are basically uncomfortable with texts which shift the focus and invite us to celebrate what *God* is going to do. In examining a complex and obscure text like the diverse collection of materials in Isaiah 24-27 ("The Isaiah Apocalypse)," we can be sure that we are closer to the intent of the prophet if we approach the text, not as a map for our future, nor as an exhortation on how we ought to live, but as a hymn—an explicit acknowledgment of God who "on that day" (Isa 24:21, 25:9; 26:1; 27:1; 27:12) will act to accomplish the divine purpose. The response which is appropriate to this material is not primarily an intellectual exercise to decipher the riddle of what every detail means, but rather a response of praise:

> O Lord, you are my God;
> I will exalt you, I will praise your name;
> for you have done wonderful things,
> plans formed of old, faithful and sure.

> (Isa 25:1)

The Hermeneutical Key

The fact that we often approach these texts with a supposition that they must have an immediate message for us today can prove to be a hermeneutical key which is quite inadequate for unlocking their meaning. An example might illustrate this most clearly. How are we to interpret Ezekiel 38-39? Set right in the midst of two pleasant scenarios of divine blessing (chapter 37, the vision of the dry bones, and chapters 40-48, the vision of the restored Temple), chapters 38-39 interject a mysterious figure by the name of Gog "of the land of Magog" (Ezek 38:2), who is to come "out the uttermost parts of the north" (38:15) and spread violence and destruction throughout the land until he and his forces are ultimately defeated and become a feast for the birds of prey (39:17-20).

Let us consider two radically different ways of approaching this text. One hermeneutic begins the exegesis of this puzzling section with the conviction that it must be talking directly to us today and giving us some needed information. The focus of attention is directed to three Hebrew words in 38:2 *rosh, meshech,* and *tubal,* and on the basis of some slight similarity of sound, these are equated with "Russia, Moscow and Tobalsk"; the "hordes from the uttermost parts of the north" (38:6) then quickly become "the communist menace from Russia." In this way, all of Ezek 38-39 is read as a literal outline of the history of the latter part of this century—as linear, predictive prophecy. The difficulties of such an approach are many, not the least being the question of why God would inspire the prophet to utter a text which could mean nothing at all to anyone for some twenty-five hundred years, since it is talking about events which are only now occurring.

The second approach explicitly refuses to read texts such as this as secret codes which contain an outline of present and future events that are available to us if we can only figure out the cipher. Rather, it calls us to come to these texts more as we would come to poetry. We are working here with the language of the imagination! The prophet deals in images and in symbols; he struggles with the resources of language available to him to try to draw us into an experiential awareness of both chaos:

> For the windows of heaven are opened,
> and the foundations of the earth tremble.
> The earth is utterly broken,
> the earth is rent asunder,
> the earth is violently shaken.

The earth staggers like a drunken man,
it sways like a hut;

(Isa 24:18-20)

and *shalom*:

. . . the mountains shall drip sweet wine,
and the hills shall flow with milk,
and all the stream beds of Judah shall flow with water;
and a fountain shall come forth from the house of the Lord
  and water the valley of Shittim

(Joel 3:18).

The prophet boldy anticipates a day to come when there will be a transformation of both the geography of the earth:

On that day his feet shall stand on the Mount of Olives . . .
and the Mount of Olives shall be split in two from east to
west by a very wide valley

(Zech 14:4)

and the very structure of the cosmos:

On that day there shall be neither cold nor frost. And
there shall be continuous day (it is known to the Lord),
not day and not night, for at evening time there shall be
light.

(Zech 14:6)

The particular images and motifs so pervasive throughout these texts are not just the personal initiatives of each individual prophet, a creation *de nouveau*. Rather, these prophets took up common ancient Near Eastern mythological and cosmic motifs and revived the language of the primordial struggle of order and chaos.[3] The victory of the Divine Warrior over the powers of chaos, the celebration banquet, the earth bursting forth with fertility and abundance, the proclamation of kingship— all these elements of the ancient Near Eastern story of creation are given an eschatological function; that is, they became the raw materials out of which the prophet could fashion a description of God's transforming activity "on that day." The great German biblical scholar H. Gunkel captured this so succinctly in the last century in his famous dictum *Endzeit gleich Urzeit,* "Primeval time is recapitulated in end-time." Thus, as we read these texts over and over, we discover that the prophets are working with a common cluster of elements which make up the "eschatological scenario": Theophany of the Divine Warrior, Conflict (cosmic, against the nations, intra-Israel), Victory and Return to Zion, Banquet, Fertility, Kingship.[4] In multiple combinations and manifestations, with amazing variations in order and detail, these elements appear in all the prophetic texts of this type, as the prophets seek to awaken the human imagination to the power of God beyond the present reality.

Now to return briefly to Ezekiel 38-39. The text exhibits signs that it originated not with the prophet Ezekiel himself but with a later prophet in a time when prophecy was well on the road to apocalyptic. Certainly there are traces that these chapters went through a complex process of development,

[3]For a simple introduction to the basic elements of Near Eastern mythology, see Michael D. Coogan, *Stories of Ancient Canaan,* (Westminster, 1978).

[4]Various scholars have outlined the eschatological scenario in slightly different ways. See, for instance, David L. Petersen, *Late Israelite Prophecy,* (Scholars Press, 1977), especially p. 17, and Donald E. Gowan, *Eschatology in the Old Testament,* (Fortress, 1986), especially p. 10.

perhaps beginning from a central core in Ezek 39:1-8. What is clear is that the defeat of "Gog from the land of Magog," must be read in the context of the total eschatological scenario. This fierce creature who brings war, bloodshed and panic even on the day when "my people Israel are dwelling securely" (38:14) is an embodiment, a concrete image of all the forces of evil, all that stands in opposition to order, peace and harmony. In contrast to the optimism of chapters 34-37, the prophet of these chapters is convinced that the final onslaught of evil is still to come. The present is not the fulfillment of all God's promises; a time of terror, violence and devastation lies ahead. *Shalom* will not come easily; the power of evil will not die without a final struggle. But the concluding prophetic word is one of consolation. Though Gog will come "like a cloud covering the land" (38:16), it is *God* who has brought him for a purpose: "so that the nations may know me, when through you, O Gog, I vindicate my holiness before their eyes" (38:16). The final result will be that "the house of Israel shall know that I am their God from that day forward" (39:22).

"The Great And Terrible Day" (Joel 2:31)

Throughout the Middle Ages and up until the liturgical reform of the 1950s, one of the most powerful texts in shaping the Catholic imagination with regard to the future was the twelfth century Latin hymn, *Dies Irae, dies Illa,* "Day of wrath, that dreadful day." (In an indirect way, the text influenced the visual imagination of the western world even more widely in that it was the source of inspiration for Michelangelo's fresco of the Last Judgement). Certain elements of the hymn actually do speak of the last day "when heaven and earth shall pass away" (verse 1). But, when the plaintive Gregorian chant was sung as the Sequence at a Funeral Mass, popular piety left little room for doubt that the "great accounting day" was the day of the individual judgement of the deceased before "the King of dreadful majesty" (verse 8). What is less well known is that much of the language of the hymn is drawn from the biblical prophets, specifically Zeph 1:14-16 and Joel 2:28-31 and that in Joel, for instance, "the great and terrible day of the Lord" is not the provenance of the individual soul at the hour of death, but the future of the world and the cosmos.

As in Ezek 38-39, this eschatological vision of the prophet Joel involves a strong and undeniable element of judgement. Starting in the first part of the book with the plague of locusts which advances "like a powerful army drawn up for battle" (Joel 2:5) and charges "like warriors, like soldiers they scale the wall" (2:7) so that "the earth quakes before them, the heavens tremble" (2:10), the historical locust plague merges almost imperceptibly into the Day of the Lord "great and very terrible, who can endure it? " (2:11). The manifestation of the Lord on that day will be preceded by "portents in the heavens and on the earth, blood and fire and columns of smoke" (2:30), the same signs (with the addition of blood) which accompanied the theophany on Mount Sinai; in addition, "the sun shall be turned to darkness, and the moon to blood, before the great and terrible day of the Lord comes" (2:31). Thus the entire cosmos is drawn into the dramatic upheaval of that final day.

Although according to Joel's description "all who call upon the name of the Lord shall be delivered" (2:32), it is the elements of judgement and wrath which predominate. The nations are gathered into the valley of Jehoshaphat to drink the eschatological cup of divine wrath. The language is heavily militaristic and intentionally ironic: the volunteers who answer the "summons-to-war,"

> Prepare war,
> stir up the mighty men.
> Let all the men of war draw near,
> let them come up
>
> (3:9)

are responding to their own destruction. The vision of peace, so well known to us from Isa 2:4 and Mic 4:3, now becomes a call to arms:

> Beat your plowshares into swords,
> and your pruning hooks into spears
>
> (3:10).

Even the weak and faint-hearted, who in traditional - Deuteronomic law would be sent back to their own houses (Deut 20:8), now must say "I am a warrior" (Joel 3:10). Many of the images are drawn from agriculture:

> Put in the sickle, for the harvest is ripe.
> Go in, tread, for the wine press is full.
> The vats overflow, for their wickedness is great
>
> (3:13);

but now they are images not of fertility but of destruction. The summons is to death, not to life.

To our way of thinking there is something narrow and nationalistic, vindictive and basically unworthy in a vision of the future which not only includes the judgement of the nations, but seems to gloat over their destruction. Our difficulty with this aspect of the eschatological scenario raises many of the same questions which surfaced when we examined the image of God as Divine Warrior (see pp. 83-90). There are no easy answers here either, but I will add two additional reflections to what was said earlier.

Though the judgement of the nations is a component of the eschatological scenario, this judgement is not simply arbitrary nor a capricious exercise of divine wrath. The nations are judged because "their wickedness is great" (Joel 3:13); they are punished because of what they have done to "my people and my heritage Israel, because they have scattered them among the nations, and have divided up my land and have cast lots for my people . . ." (3:2-3 with an additional expansion in verses 4-8). "The nations" embody the forces of wickedness and sin; they have become almost a cosmic image for evil (as is "Leviathan the fleeing serpent"—Isa 27:1). Their punishment and ultimate destruction is necessary as the final manifestation of justice.

Even for the nations, judgement is not the final word. Deutero-Zechariah makes place in the eschatological scenario for "every one that survives of all the nations that have come against Jerusalem" (Zech 14:16) as he envisions the remnant of the nations coming to Jerusalem to acknowledge the Lord in celebration. The final vision is of the Lord as "king over all the earth; on that day the Lord will be one and his name one" (Zech 14:9). This final doxological statement seems to be an early exegesis of Israel's great confession of faith, the *Shema*: "Hear, O Israel, the Lord our God is one Lord" (Deut 6:4). It is in the age to come that the *Shema* will be fully realized and God's exclusive suzerainty will be acknowledged by all the nations of the earth as they "go up year after year to worship the King, the Lord of hosts" (Zech 14:16).

"Behold I Create New Heavens And a New Earth" (Isa 65:17)

In the magnificent poem in Isa 65:17-25, Third Isaiah invites us to move beyond judgement in the eschatological scenario to catch a glimpse of the "new heavens and new earth" of the future. In many ways, the prophet's vision turns out to be rather cautious and subdued. We are presented with a transformed world which is surprisingly like the world as we now know it; certainly the future as envisioned here has not been totally removed to an ethereal, spiritual realm.

The future is to be an act of divine creativity: "I create new heavens and a new earth . . . I create Jerusalem" (65:17, 18). Later apocalyptic would tend to focus much more specifically on the cosmic upheaval, the radical break by which this age would end and the new heavens and earth begin (compare 2 Pet 3:10 "the heavens will pass away with a loud noise, and the elements will be dissolved with fire)." But Third Isaiah says nothing of the destruction of this world. Rather, he moves with surprising alacrity from the expansive "new heavens and a new earth" to the specific "I create Jerusalem." His primary eschatological symbol is a particular place and geographical entity, a place of infants and elderly, of houses and vineyards, of labor and childbirth, of animals wild and tame. It is a world which still knows death, but a death which comes only at its appropriate time. No longer shall death overstep its bounds to take "an infant that lives but a few days" (65:20); "anyone who fails to live a hundred years will be considered as accursed" (65:20b, according to the NEB translation)—a full hundred years, not just the traditional threescore and ten (Ps 90:10)! The judgement oracle of the earlier prophet Zephaniah, "Though they build houses, they shall not inhabit them; though they plant vineyards, they shall not drink wine from them" (Zeph 1:13), is totally reversed, "They shall build houses and inhabit them; they shall plant vineyards and eat their fruit" (65:21). Yet, this is not the extravagant apocalyptic dream where "one vine will give a thousand branches, and one branch a thousand clusters, and one cluster a thousand grapes" (2 Baruch 29:5), where "the treasury of manna will come down again from on high" (2 Bar 29:8); this is still the world of human labor, a labor that does not strive in vain but with the assurance that "my chosen shall long enjoy the work of their hands" (Isa 65:22-23). The prophet's vision of the future will only reach fulfillment when the lion no longer stalks prey for his supper and the wolf and the lamb can together live in harmony and without fear, a concrete manifestation that "they shall not hurt or destroy in all my holy mountain" (65:25).

In this vision, Third Isaiah presents a poetic act of imagination. Its truth does not lie on the level of a pragmatic program for action, nor does its authenticity depend upon the zoologist's opinion about the likelihood of convincing the lion to change its diet! This is a vision—a vision of the future. But, to acknowledge that this is a vision of the future is not to deny that it both can, and necessarily does, impinge on our understanding of the present. When the prophet names some of the elements of a "new heavens and a new earth," he is revealing something about the present as well as about the future; we are confronted by dimensions of this future which are absent from our world here and now. To envision, for instance, the future as a time when "they shall not hurt or destroy in all my holy mountain" is, in essence, a critique of present realities and a signpost to guide us on the road to the future.

"I Will Pour Out My Spirit" (Joel 2:28)

An important though somewhat surprising component of
the eschatological age is the promise of a revitalization of
prophecy itself, either as a gift given to many (Joel 2:28), or in
the person of a single prophet yet to come (Mal 4:5). I say
surprising component for it is precisely in these late prophetic
texts that we find the most negative critique of prophecy in
the whole of Scripture. Although it is doubtful that we can
recover fully the concrete historical situation which gave rise
to a text such as Zech 13:2-6 for instance, its polemical intent
is clear: "on that day . . . I remove from the land the prophets
and the unclean spirit . . . every prophet will be ashamed of
his vision when he prophesies" (Zech 13:2, 4). In this anti-
prophetic diatribe, the old motifs of prophecy are taken up for
the sole purpose of rejecting them: the words of Amos 7:14, "I
am no prophet," become a literal statement of fact (13:5); the
marks of prophetic activity—vision, dress (the hairy mantle 1
Kgs 19:2, 2 Kgs 2:13), the ecstatic wounds (1 Kgs 18:28)—are
all mocked. Anyone who dares to prophesy risks suffering the
penalty of death which the Law had prescribed for the wicked
son (Deut 13:1-11, 21:18-21). To the author of this text,
prophecy itself, at least as it comes from one group of those
calling themselves prophets, was to be condemned.

However, in the age to come, prophecy will once again be a
positive and living phenomenon as God fulfills the promise,
"It will come to pass afterward, that I will pour out my spirit
on all flesh" (Joel 2:28). It has often been noted that in
post-exilic theological thought there was an increased emphasis
on the role of the Spirit.[5] When Third Isaiah retells the Exodus

[5]Richard J. Sklba, "Until the Spirit from on High is Poured Out on Us' " (Isa

story, he introduces the Spirit three times (63:10, 11, 14); similarly, when the long Deuteronomic prayer in Neh 9 recounts the Wilderness story, it adds the Spirit (9:20) to the traditional gifts of manna and water. In rebuilding the Temple, Zerubbabel will act "not by might, nor by power, but by my Spirit" (Zech 4:6); the Servant brings the deliverance of the Jubilee Year because "the Spirit of the Lord God is upon me" (Isa 61:1). For Ezekiel, the day will come when "I will not hide my face any more from them, when I pour out my Spirit upon the house of Israel" (Ezek 39:29).

It is the prophet Joel who is most specific about naming what this outpouring of the Spirit will entail:

> your sons and daughters shall prophesy,
> your old men shall dream dreams,
> and your young men shall see visions
>
> (Joel 2:28).

The Spirit is to be poured out "on all flesh." It is the spirit of prophecy which will break the barriers of sex ("your sons and your daughters"), age ("your old men . . . and your young men"), and social status ("the menservants and maidservants"). In the last days, the wish of Moses in the desert will be fulfilled: "Would that all the people were prophets, that the Lord would put his spirit upon them!" (Num 11:29).

In Malachi, rather than the outpouring of the spirit of prophecy on all, the promise is of a single prophet to come: "Behold, I send my messenger to prepare the way before me" (Mal 3:1). In the Persian period, messenger *(malach)* increasingly becomes a term which replaces *nabi'*, "prophet" (Isa

32:15): Reflections on the Role of the Spirit in the Exile," *Catholic Biblical Quarterly* 46, 1984, pp 1-17.

42:19; 44:26; 63:9; Hag 1:13). In a later apocalyptic colophon (Mal 4:4-5) which is perhaps meant to serve as an appendix to the entire prophetic collection, both the time and the identity of this messenger are further specified. Elijah, who did not die but was "taken" to heaven (2 Kgs 2:11) in his fiery chariot, becomes the prophet who will return "before the great and terrible day of the Lord" (4:5), "to turn the hearts of fathers to their children and the hearts of children to their fathers" (4:6). In the early Greek translations of this verse, the prophetic task of reconciliation reaches even beyond the confines of the family: "Elias . . . shall turn again the heart of the father to the son, and the heart of people to their neighbors." Thus, the final manifestation of the prophetic spirit is to bring about mutuality, reconciliation and harmony among all.

"He Will Swallow Up Death Forever" (Isa 25:8)

Any in-depth reflection on the human condition and any vision which directs our gaze to the future must confront the reality of death. Throughout most of the Old Testament, the Israelite people shared the common worldview which permeated the cultures of the ancient Near East; they accepted the fundamental "given" that

> when the gods created human beings
> they allotted them death,
> but life the gods retained
> in their own keeping.
>
> (Gilgamesh Epic)

The ancients observed that at death the breath, the vital life-giving force, left the human body. After death, there was only a shadowy existence in Sheol, "the land of gloom and deep darkness . . . the land of gloom and chaos, where light is as darkness" (Job 10:21-22). "The dead know nothing" (Ecc 9:5), not even God; as the psalmist laments, "in death there is no remembrance of you; in Sheol who can give you praise?" (Ps 6:5). Throughout most of the Old Testament, the reward for the one who leads a "good life" must come in *this life*: "if you obey the voice of the Lord your God . . . all these blessings will come upon you . . . the Lord will make you abound in prosperity, in the fruit of your body, and in the fruit of your cattle, and in the fruit of your ground, within the land which the Lord swore to your fathers to give you . . . to establish you as a people holy to himself . . . the Lord will cause your enemies who rise against you to be defeated before you" (Deut 28:1, 7, 9, 11).

This traditional Old Testament worldview is so totally different from our Christian confession, "I believe in the resurrection of the body and the life everlasting" (the Apostles' Creed), that it may be difficult, at first glance, to see the connecting links. It is clear that by the time of Jesus certain streams of Jewish theology had come to a radically new understanding of these issues. Though the more theologically conservative Sadducees continued to maintain "that there is no resurrection, nor angel, nor spirit" (Acts 23:8), the more theologically progressive Pharisees "acknowledge them all" (Acts 23:8) and the apostle Paul readily confesses "I am a Pharisee . . . with respect to the hope and the resurrection of the dead" (Acts 23:6). Precisely *how*, in the last centuries of the pre-Christian era, the Jewish people came to faith in the power of God as Lord over both life and death, and how they came to express this faith in the language of resurrection, immortality and eternal life, is an extremely complex question and one which we will probably never be able to answer fully. What is clear is that by the second century BC, we can point to specific texts which articulate a new understanding: Dan 12:2 "and many of those who sleep in the dust of the earth shall awake . . . " and 2 Mac 7:9 "the King of the universe will raise us up to an everlasting renewal of life."

In order to examine the process which culminated in this new understanding, we turn for a final look at the collection of post-exilic prophetic texts which are the nucleus of this chapter. It is within the context of these eschatological visions of the future that the prophets voice the first "intimations of immortality." (A similar inchoate reaching out toward a future beyond death may also be hinted at in some of the post-exilic psalms, notably Ps 16:10; 49:14-15; 73:24). In particular, the unnamed prophet of the Isaiah Apocalypse (Isa 24-27) includes victory over death itself as one of the components in the final manifestation of God's salvific power.

The first text to consider is Isa 26:19:

> Your dead shall live, their bodies shall rise.
> O dwellers in the dust, awake and sing for joy!
> For your dew is dew of light,
> and on the land of the shades you will let it fall.

The reading of this text is difficult; the Hebrew is virtually unintelligible, and all translators have to make slight emendations (as can be seen when various English translations are compared). For a fuller exegesis of this verse and all its problems, it will be necessary to refer to more detailed commentaries. The difficulties with this text are compounded by the fact that it is not clear how, or how closely, 26:19 should be related to the verses preceding and following (note, for instance, the apparent contradiction with 26:14). It is obvious that we do not have here an apologetic discourse, giving cogent reasons for or arguing the possibility of life after death. Rather, the prophet is employing a series of images: the dew—so vital and life-giving in the parched summer months in Palestine—light, and awakening. The Lord's dew is "a dew of light" which falls upon "the dwellers in the dust" so that the "dead shall live."

The second passage for consideration is Isa 25:6-8:

> On this mountain the Lord of hosts will make for all peoples a feast of fat things. . . . And he will destroy on this mountain the covering that is cast over all peoples, the veil that is spread over all nations. He will swallow up death for ever, and the Lord God will wipe away tears from all faces, and the reproach of his people he will take away from the earth; for the Lord has spoken.

The verse which is central to our concerns, "He [God] will swallow up death for ever" (25:8), is usually taken to be a secondary addition, although it is hard to determine this conclusively. In this vision, "all peoples" flock to the sacred mountain, gathering now not for judgement and destruction, but for a superabundant feast (the Hebrew words here have a poetic assonance impossible to capture in English, *shemanim memuḥayim*, "delicious meats," *shemarim mezuqqaqim*, "choicest wines"). As the people devour the rich food and drink, the Lord will utterly destroy even death itself. There is powerful irony here. In ancient Near Eastern thought *Mot* "death" is a devouring beast; in Isaiah 5:14 we read: "Sheol has enlarged its appetite and opened its mouth beyond measure." The prophet continues this mythic image even as he totally reverses it; on the last day the Lord "will *swallow up* death forever."

From one perspective these two verses offer very little;

there is so much that they do not say, much less try to explain. In the language of imagery and symbol, these anonymous prophets have expressed their conviction that the power of God reaches even to the realm of death itself. For it is only when death, the ultimate enemy, is destroyed that "the Lord God will wipe away tears from all faces" (25:8). Then, on that day, it will be said:

> Lo, this is our God; we have waited for him
> that he might save us.
> This is the Lord; we have waited for him;
> let us be glad and rejoice in his salvation.

(Isa 25:9)

7

GOD PRESENT AND ABSENT

> The Old Testament knows of a God who is near as well as far
> off, a God who reveals himself and who hides himself, a God
> who is humanly comprehensible and at the same time menacing,
> contradictory, unpredictable and incomprehensible. It is in such
> complexity and contrariety, however, sometimes in one form
> and sometimes in another that we experience life itself and it is
> in such complexity that we also experience God.[1]

Throughout the experience of the suffering of the Exile, the
joy and expectation of the Restoration, the disillusionment of
the post-exilic community, the prophets spoke to the people
about a God who is "near as well as far off." In the book of
Jeremiah, the question is put directly:

> "Am I a God at hand, says the Lord,
> and not a God afar off?"
>
> (Jer 23:23)

In the Hebrew text, this rhetorical question is formulated so as
to call forth a negative answer—no, God is not at hand or

[1]Herbert Haag, from his farewell discourse on retiring from the University of
Tübingen (1980), quoted by Bruce Vawter, "The God of Hebrew Scriptures"
Biblical Theology Bulletin, 12, 1982, p. 6.

near: God is not a local deity whom one can manipulate and control, or from whom one might manage to hide. However, the Greek translation of this verse makes a positive statement, totally inverting the meaning, "I am a God at hand, says the Lord, and not a God far off." This Jeremiah text must, of course, be interpreted as a whole in light of its specific context in a discussion of the issue of true and false prophecy,[2] but for our purposes here, this verse does serve to pose a critical question in stark and unavoidable terms.

One of the most fundamental issues of spirituality and a question for all of us in varying ways and at different stages of our faith journey is simply this: how do we recognize the presence of God? Is the God whom we know a God who is near, or a God who is far off? When we feel the absence and distance of God, how do we explain this? In what sense can we talk of a God who is both present and absent—does this expression have any meaning, or is it just a play on words, a confusing paradox? These are often among the first questions to surface at a time of retreat, when entering into spiritual direction, in an RCIA class, or in a Cursillo or Antioch weekend—or just at home amidst the bustle of daily concerns. In the course of our lives we can be convinced that we have come to some answers, only to find that the question breaks open anew in times of personal crisis.

Contemporary theologians use the more abstract and theoretical terms of immanence and transcendence to express the same basic tension: how is it possible to maintain the dialectic between a God who is near, known, and present (immanent)

[2]Werner E. Lemke, "The Near and the Distant God: A Study of Jeremiah 23:23-24 in its Biblical Theological Context," *Journal of Biblical Literature* 100, 1981, pp 541-55.

and a God who is distant, other, and hidden (transcendent)? This is not simply an abstract speculation for philosophers and theologians; it has intensely practical ramifications. If our God is totally "our there" or "up there," this can easily lead to an other-worldly orientation in which God can only be found in heavenly things (in prayer, liturgy, penance, retreat, "church" activities) so that every day "this-worldly" concerns seem totally unimportant, or at least separate from the realm of God. But an understanding of God as totally immanent and present can lead to a type of pantheism, or a God who is confined to the limitations of our own imagination and understanding. A few years ago, the biblical theologian Samuel Terrien tried to capture both elements in the phrase "the Elusive Presence"; indeed he suggested that this concept of "elusive presence" could be the core and unifying focus of an all-embracing theology of both Old and New Testament, the very heart of biblical theology.[3]

God—Transcendent And Immanent

By the time of the Exile, there already existed a rich tradition and language to speak of the transcendent aspect of God. For instance, the book of Isaiah repeatedly names God as "the Holy One." In Isaiah's vision in chapter 6, the prophet saw the Lord "sitting upon a throne, high and lifted up, and his train filled the Temple" (Isa 6:1). The seraphim in the choir of praise in the heavenly court cried to one another, "Holy, holy, holy is the Lord of hosts; the whole earth is full of his glory"

[3]Samuel Terrien, *The Elusive Presence: The Heart of Biblical Theology*, (Harper & Row, 1978).

(Isa 6:3). The holiness acclaimed here does not correspond exactly to our sense of an ethical and moral purity; rather, it is the quality of absolute distinctiveness and otherness. Yet, although God is other and separate, "his glory" fills the earth; this glory, often symbolized by the cloud (as in the desert wanderings Ex 24:15, in the Tent of Meeting Ex 40:34), is that aspect of God which is immanent and present on earth. But, to return to Isaiah 6, the experience of the transcendence of the divine arouses in the prophet an acute and painful awareness of the chasm which separates any human person from the holy, "Woe is me! For I am lost; for I am a man of unclean lips, and I dwell in the midst of a people of unclean lips; for my eyes have seen the king, the Lord of hosts" (Isa 6:5). In the early part of this century, in a classic essay,[4] Rudolph Otto characterized this double aspect of the holy: it is both a *mysterium tremendum*, dangerous and frightening, and also a *mysterium fascinans*, exercising a compelling attraction and power to entice. In these few verses Isaiah has captured the fundamental nature of all genuine religious experience, the existential awareness that God is no "cosmic buddy."[5]

Yet along with this awesome awareness of holiness, the biblical authors had an equally vivid sense of the nearness of God. In a radical move, these two truths are brought together in a single powerful statement, "The Holy One in your midst" (Hos 11:9, Isa 12:6). This is a nearness which was experienced in the thunder, cloud and fire of the theophany at Mt. Sinai (Ex 19: 16-20) and then in the cloud which accompanied the people during the desert wanderings and filled the Tent of

[4]Rudolf Otto, *The Idea of the Holy*, (Oxford University Press, 1923).

[5]The phrase comes from William Holladay, *Isaiah: Scroll of a Prophetic Heritage*, (Eerdmans, 1978), p. 31.

Meeting. For the author of Deuteronomy, it was possible to speak of God's nearness because of the gift of God's self-disclosure in the Law (Torah); Israel could rejoice and boast: "for what other nation is there that has a god so near to it as the Lord our God is to us?" (Deut 4:7). The Yahwist storyteller is remarkably successful in giving a vivid sense of the nearness of God by the bold use of anthropomorphisms: God is intimately present, walking in the garden in the cool of the evening (Gen 3:8), shutting up the door of the ark (Gen 7:16). Furthermore, the Jewish rabbi and philosopher Abraham Heschel has called attention to the "passionate" language ascribed to God, particularly by the prophets: "He [God] is moved and affected by what happens in the world, and reacts accordingly. Events and human actions arouse in Him joy or sorrow, pleasure or wrath. He is not conceived as judging the world in detachment. He reacts in an intimate and subjective manner."[6] This is the language of a God who is near and present.

With the building of the Temple at the time of David and Solomon, the critical question became how to maintain the dialectic between the divine presence to Israel and the divine freedom from Israel. On the one hand, the Temple, "the house of the Lord" in the Hebrew text, was the locus of divine presence. Like all temples in the ancient Near East, it was located on a sacred mountain, Mount Zion "where the Lord will dwell forever" (Ps 68:16). Thus, for the psalmist, to enter the Temple was to come into the divine presence "to behold the beauty of the Lord" (Ps 27:4). Yet, on the other hand, there was a profound recognition that God cannot be contained in the Temple: "But will God indeed dwell on the earth?

[6]Abraham Heschel, *The Prophets*, (Harper & Row, 1962), p. 224.

Behold, heaven and the highest heaven cannot contain you; how much less this house which I have built?" (1 Kgs 8:27). Deuteronomy develops a "theology of the name" to deal in a theologically sophisticated way with this mystery: though God is in heaven, yet his *name* is set in the Temple, the place of which it is said, "My name shall be there" (1 Kgs 8:29-30). Lest the presence in the Temple be too easily controlled and domesticated, the Priestly theologians hesitated to talk in ordinary everyday vocabulary of God "dwelling" in the - Temple; rather, they chose a special verb *shkn*, "to tent," to express the temporary, fluid nature of the divine presence— again, an attempt to preserve the element of divine freedom.

Perhaps the most sustained and careful attempt to grapple with this mystery is the text in Ex 33:18-23, a complex passage which brings together many different strands of reflection.[7] Although slightly earlier in the same chapter we are told that "the Lord used to speak to Moses face to face, as a man speaks to his friend" (33:11), the conclusion of the chapter serves as a salutary corrective to any assumption of the ready accessibility of the divine. Moses begs to see the glory of the Lord (33:18) and is informed that no one can see the face of God and live. In the end, God both consents and refuses the request: "I will put you in a cleft of the rock, and I will cover you with my hand until I have passed by; then I will take away my hand, and you shall see my back; but my face shall not be seen" (33:22-23). There is disclosure but God still remains apart. The Rabbis brought together this passage and the text in Isaiah 6 which we considered earlier: Isaiah who "saw the Lord sitting on the

[7]For a fuller exegesis of this important passage, see Walter Brueggemann, "The Crisis and Promise of Presence in Israel," *Horizons in Biblical Theology*, I, 1979, pp 47-86.

throne" and Moses who saw only the Lord's back. The Rabbis asked: "Which of these was the greater prophet?" Their answer: Moses, because he did not see God, while Isaiah was the lesser prophet because he thought he did see God!

Absence: Presence In Judgement

It is against the background of this pre-exilic theological understanding of the presence of God as focused in Temple and cult that we can appreciate the terrible crisis of faith which the Exile precipitated. For the exiles, more painful than any physical hardship was the overwhelming sense that they were cut off from God and the traditional means of access to the divine realm (Temple, sacrifice, pilgrimage). In a graphic manner, Ezekiel sees in a vision (chapter 8-11) that the abominations and defilements in the Temple have driven God from the sanctuary. With terrifying irony, the people justify their actions saying "The Lord does not see us, the Lord has forsaken the land" (Ezek 8:12), while it is precisely because the Lord *does see* that he departs from the land. Thus, in Babylon, the exiles experience the absence of their God; they lament, "my way is hid from the Lord, and my right is disregarded by my God" (Isa 40:27), "the Lord has forsaken me, my Lord has forgotten me" (Isa 49:14). It was not just geographical distance which lay behind the cry "How shall we sing the Lord's songs in a foreign land?" (Ps 137:4), but the terrifying possibility that God had totally withdrawn and was no longer accessible: "You have wrapped yourself with a cloud so that no prayer can pass through" (Lam 3:44).

How do the prophets respond to the theological challenge implicit in these laments? They take up the question with absolute seriousness, offering no easy answers, no ready assurance that "Oh yes, things are really as they were before, God is always with us." They dismiss any attempt at explanation for the absence which would shift the blame to the Lord's impotence or fickleness in abandoning his people. Rather, the prophetic word both acknowledges and interprets the meaning of this absence. For the prophets, absence is not just negative; in the supreme paradox, it must be seen as God's presence, a presence in judgement.

Many years earlier, the prophet Micah had proclaimed that for those "who hate the good and love the evil" (Mic 3:2), the day would come when "they will cry to the Lord, but he will not answer them; he will hide his face from them at that time, because they have made their deeds evil." (Mic 3:4). In the events of exile, these words are fulfilled: "for I have hidden my face from this city because of their wickedness" (Jer 33:5). Similarly in Deuteronomy, the Lord anticipates a day when "my anger will be kindled against them . . . and I will forsake them and hide my face from them, and they will be devoured; and many evils and troubles will come upon them, so that they will say in that day, "Have not these evils come upon us because our God is not among us?" And I will surely hide my face in that day on account of all the evil which they have done" (Deut 31:17-18). God is still free and sovereign; God has freely chosen to hide his face, to be absent in judgement as a just response to the unfaithfulness of the people.

The prophet's treatment of the absence of God as experienced in the historical reality of the Exile adds a new dimension to an ancient theme. In some of the oldest religious texts from the civilizations which surrounded Israel, we find the individual, particularly in a time of suffering, questioning the god's absence: "How long, O my lady, will you be angry and your face be turned away?" (Prayer to Ishtar, second millenium BC). The psalmists, too, voice their feeling of being cut off from the presence of God, experiencing only silence even within the sacred confines of the Temple; they question, "why do you hide your face from me?" (Ps 88:14).[8] But for the prophets, the absence of God is not just a general and universal human experience of the hiddenness and incomprehensibility of the divine (for further discussion of this aspect, see pp. 183-185). That absence can also be punishment for sinfulness and the lived experience of judgement is a key and enduring prophetic revelation.

This conviction that there is an absence of God which is directly linked to human sinfulness provides the hermeneutical key (particularly for Third Isaiah and Malachi) which explains the continuing dilemma of the post-exilic situation. Why is God still absent, even after the exiles had returned to the land and the Temple had been rebuilt? In giving his answer, Third Isaiah first negates the false assumption of the people: "Behold, the Lord's hand is not shortened, that it cannot save, or his ear dull, that it cannot hear" (Isa 59:1); then he gives the prophetic word of interpretation: "but your iniquities have made a separation between you and your God, and your sins have hid his face from you, so that he does not hear" (59:2). Similarly, in the time of Malachi when the people ask "where is the God of justice?" (Mal 2:17), the prophet demands that they look to the existing evils in their society (failure of the priests to perform their duties, exploitation of the poor, withholding of tithes, marriage with foreign wives) for their answer.

---

[8]For further discussion and theological reflection on this motif of God "hiding his face," see Samuel E. Ballentine, *The Hidden God: The Hiding of the Face of God in the Old Testament*, (Oxford University Press, 1983), especially pp 157-63.

But for the prophets, the absence of God is never the final answer, the normal state. The final word is presence, not absence. The God whose face is hidden in judgement will make known his compassion when the time of judgement is past:

> For a brief moment I forsook you,
> but with great compassion I will gather you.
> In overflowing wrath for a moment,
> I hide my face from you,
> but with everlasting love
> I will have compassion on you
> says the Lord the redeemer.
> (Isa 54:7-8)

Presence In The Temple

What about the presence of God in the Temple? Surprisingly, concern for the Temple is a central theme for three of the prophets of our period: Ezekiel, Haggai and Zechariah. I say surprisingly, as it is in these three prophets that the divergent streams of prophecy and cult come together in what is a hitherto unprecedented manner. Although, as we have noted already (pp. 119-121), it is far too simplistic to say that any of the prophets were opposed on principle to cultic worship, it is hard to imagine Amos or Jeremiah, for instance, speaking in support of a temple rebuilding program as insistently as do Haggai or Zechariah.

More than any other prophet, Ezekiel attempted to put into words the indescribable presence of God as experienced in the Temple; the results of this bold initiative (especially in chapters 1-3) strike us as obscure, weird, even terrifying. St. Jerome tells us that some Rabbis issued the equivalent of a Surgeon

General's warning to all who approach this book—"may be dangerous to your health"; thus, the various rabbinic dicta that Ezekiel wrote was not to be read by anyone under age 30, or without the guidance of a teacher!

As a priest, Ezekiel's interest was focused on the Temple. His language is that of the priestly circles—cloud, cherubim, ark, throne, fire and above all the terminology "glory" to describe the ineffable presence of the divine in the Temple. Although concrete objects (the four creatures, a complicated system of wheels, a sapphire throne) are described in the two great visions of chapters 1-3 and 8-11, the objects go beyond the realm of logic and ordinary sense experience. Yet much of this description which seems so strange and new to us was, in fact, firmly rooted in traditional ancient Near Eastern temple iconography. The highly formulaic language, the repetition of phrases, the redundancy of certain expressions (although perhaps reflecting also the complex literary history of these chapters) is itself indicative of the inadequacy of language to describe the experience. Ezekiel moves in his description from the four creatures each with four faces (the cherubim) to the moving chariot-throne , and finally to a figure of brightness and fire; at this point, words fail, or are at least three-times removed—"such was the appearance/of the likeness/of the glory/of the Lord" (1:28).

In his vision in chapters 8:1-11:25, the prophet describes how the glory of the Lord and the attendant cherubim departed from the sanctuary in stages, moving from the threshold (9:3, 10:1-5), then out the east gate to the mountain on the east side of the city (10:18-19, 11:22-23). The departure is clearly a judgement on the abuses which are defiling the Temple (chapter 8). Faced with overwhelming pollution and desecration, God simply moved out, and the Temple, bereft of the divine presence, was left to face judgement.

But for Ezekiel too, this is not the final word. If God is to return, to be present again, it must be within the Temple. In a short passage in chapter 37:24-28, after the vision of the dried bones restored to new life, the prophet describes the various elements of the restoration:

> My servant David shall be king over them (37:24);

> They shall follow my ordinances and be careful to observe my statutes (37:24);

> They shall dwell in the land where your fathers dwelt (37:25)

> I will make a covenant of peace with them (37:26);

and, as the climax,

> I will set my sanctuary in the midst of them for evermore.
> My dwelling place shall be with them; and I will be their
> God and they shall be my people. Then the nations will know
> that I the Lord sanctify Israel, when my sanctuary is in the
> midst of them for evermore. (37:26-28)

This hope of God's presence and blessing is expanded in Ezekiel's final magnificent vision, which is really a "Cook's tour" of the restored Temple (chapters 40-48). After making his way with his heavenly companion around the Temple complex, Ezekiel arrives at the east gate to witness "the glory of the God of Israel" coming from the east. Lest there be any doubt about the significance of what he is seeing, he carefully explains, "the vision I saw was like the vision which I had seen when he came to destroy the city, and like the vision which I had seen by the river Chebar" (43:3). The glory enters the Temple by the east gate, "and behold, the glory of the Lord filled the temple" (43:5). To further specify, Ezekiel hears a voice, "Son of man, this is the place of my throne and the place of the soles of my feet, where I will dwell in the midst of the people of Israel forever." (43:7). The glory which is focused in the Temple in fact fills the whole city, so that the lengthy vision ends with the assurance that in the future the city of Jerusalem shall be renamed "The Lord is there" (48:35).

Rebuilding the Temple: Haggai and Zechariah

Like Ezekiel, the prophets Haggai and Zechariah are firmly rooted in this Temple-centered tradition. For Haggai in particular, the presence of the Lord with the restored community is inextricably tied to the rebuilding of the Temple. Almost twenty years after returning to the land, the people have rebuilt their own houses, but the house of God lies in ruins (1:4). The failure to rebuild the Temple is not just a simple matter of economics, a debatable item in the ranking of priorities for the state public works program. Within the worldview of ancient temple theology (a worldview shared by Haggai), the presence of the deity in the Temple is a prerequisite for the fertility of the land: "Because of my house that lies in ruins ... therefore, the heavens above you have withheld the dew, and the earth has withheld its produce" (1:9-10). When the Temple is completed, "the latter splendor of this house shall be greater than the former ... and in this place I will give prosperity, says the Lord of hosts" (2:9); then will come *shalom*, not just peace, but as the RSV rightly translates, "prosperity."

Finally, there is also an eschatological, a not-yet, still-to-be-expected, dimension to the Temple rebuilding. The poets of old had vividly described how the earth once "reeled and rocked; the foundations of the mountains trembled" (Ps 18:7) at the coming (theophany) of the Holy One; so, in the days to come, "once again, in a little while, I will shake the heavens and the earth and the sea and the dry land; and I will shake all nations, so that the treasures of all nations shall come in, and I will fill this house with splendor, says the Lord of hosts" (Hag 2:6-7).

Zechariah, through a unique fusion of vision and oracle, gives equally strong prophetic endorsement to the Temple building project. Although Haggai and Zechariah are often taken as "twin" prophets with the same message (an impression reinforced by the way later tradition "lumps them together," e.g., Ezra 5:1), Zechariah envisions the presence of the Lord more in terms of the city Jerusalem than in terms of the Temple specifically. In the second vision of the man with a measuring line in his hand, the language of glory is transferred to the city, "Jerusalem shall be inhabited as villages without walls . . . for I will be to her a wall of fire round about, says the Lord, and I will be the glory within her." (2:4-5). In the oracle attached to this vision, the daughter of Zion is called upon to sing and rejoice "for lo, I come and will dwell in the midst of you, says the Lord" (2:10). Similarly, "I will return to Zion, and will dwell in the midst of Jerusalem, and Jerusalem shall be called the faithful city, and the mountain of the Lord of hosts, the holy mountain" (8:3). Yet, it is specifically on the rebuilding of the Temple that Zechariah stakes his very authenticity as a prophet; when it is completed, "then you will know that the Lord of hosts has sent me to you" (Zech 4:9, 6:15).

This insistence on Temple and cult, the close linking of the presence of God to the actual physical rebuilding of the Temple is a distinctive feature of the spirituality of Ezekiel, Haggai and Zechariah. It is the one aspect of these prophets which is most foreign to us. Somehow it seems crassly - materialistic—an institution built with, and supported by, Persian money is so "establishment." We ask, can the presence of God be guaranteed so surely? Is this not a return to the false self-confidence that Jeremiah castigated, the temptation to think that the mere insistence "this is the temple of the Lord, the temple of the Lord" (Jer 7:4) insures divine presence and beneficence?

Even to ask these questions in this way raises more issues than can be dealt with here. We need to recall again, as we saw in the last chapter, that these same prophets do make a link between righteousness and justice and the presence of God; there are no automatic guarantees. If we think back to the visions of Zechariah 5, we can see that there is a fundamental understanding that God can only dwell with a people purged of wickedness, particularly the crimes of economic and social exploitation. Other prophets continued to press the question. It is taken up in the most radical form as a direct oracle from the Lord:

> Thus says the Lord:
> Heaven is my throne
> and the earth is my footstool;
> what is the house which you would build for me,
> and what is the place of my rest?
> All these things my hand has made,
> and so all these things are mine, says the Lord.
> But this is the man to whom I will look,
> he that is humble and contrite in spirit,
> and trembles at my word.
> (Isa 66:1-2)

Given the strong personal and social justice orientation of much of contemporary spirituality, we are predisposed to believe that the Lord does look with favor not upon the mere physical structure of temple/church, but upon the person who is "humble and contrite in spirit, and trembles at my word" (Isa 66:2). However, it is important that we also hear the voices of Ezekiel, Haggai, and Zechariah—their confidence that the institutions of Temple, cult and priesthood can be the vehicle of divine presence. We readily acknowledge that a spirituality which finds God primarily in the established institutions of cult and temple faces the ever-present temptation to domestication and self-confidence, the risk of blithely assuming that the divine can be ever at our beck and call. But, at a particular time in history, in the latter quarter of the sixth century B.C., it was precisely the prophetic voice of stability and pragmatism, the insistence upon the practical steps of Temple rebuilding, which enabled the post-exilic community to reestablish itself and face the demands of living under foreign domination. This spirituality, focused on the centrality and richness of Temple and Temple worship, came to fullest expression in the two books of the Chronicler and continued to live with vigor and warmth throughout subsequent centuries (e.g., 1 Mac 14:29; 2 Mac 13:10; 14:29; 2:16-18; Tobit 13:3-8; 14:5; Sir 35:1-11, 50:1-21).Today these prophetic texts still challenge us to re-examine our readiness to admit the presence of God in all aspects of life, even those areas which can seem the most institutional and established.

Presence In Suffering

While the prophets Haggai, Zechariah and Ezekiel focused their attention on the Lord's presence in the Temple, Second Isaiah looked elsewhere in search of the divine. For this prophet, the presence and action of God is not to be found in the stability and splendor of the cult, but, in some mysterious way, in an enigmatic figure, "my servant," who suffers so terribly that he is scarcely recognized as human, but ultimately is vindicated and exalted.

Since these particular passages have not been discussed elsewhere, let me begin with a few words of introduction to the four specific poems in Second Isaiah which are commonly designated as "the Suffering Servant Songs." Scholars are divided in opinion as to whether they are the work of the same prophet who wrote the rest of chapters 40-55 or whether they may have had a different origin; in any case, these four passages form a clearly recognizable body of material. Each describes, in a different way, a figure identified as "my servant":

> Isa 42:1-4: "He will bring forth justice to the nations" (vs 1)
> Isa 49:1-6: "I will give you as a light to the nations" (vs 6)
> Isa 50:4-9: "I gave my back to the smiters" (vs 6)
> Isa 52:13-53:12: "He was despised, and we esteemed him not" (vs 3)

These four short passages contain some of the most loved, but also the most puzzling verses in the whole of the Old Testament. It seems as if every few years a lengthy article or even a book is written by a scholar just to survey the hundreds of pages written by other scholars on these verses.[9] In fact, earlier in this century, the renowned and learned English biblical scholar S.R. Driver worked for years writing a lengthy commentary on the book of Isaiah, but was finally compelled to abandon the project because he couldn't decide how to

---

[9]For a helpful survey of this vast literature, see R.N. Whybray, *The Second Isaiah*, Old Testament Guides, (JSOT Press, 1983), pp 65-78.

interpret these passages! I mention some of these difficulties at the beginning of our discussion, not to discourage or to burden the reader unduly, but to emphasize that we cannot hope in a few pages to undertake a full and detailed study of these passages—much less to solve all the problems. Here, most particularly, the reader is invited to read the biblical text prayerfully and slowly, and to refer to other standard commentaries for a fuller discussion.

As we ponder these word-pictures of the Servant, the key question quickly becomes "*Who* is this Servant?" Who is this unnamed figure who is given such an exalted mission to the nations but who also suffers so horribly and ignominiously? We are not, of course, the first to ask the question; almost two thousand years ago, an Ethiopian eunuch read verses 7-8 of chapter 53: "Like a lamb that is led to its slaughter, or a sheep that before its shearers is dumb . . . ," and was puzzled as to the identity of this figure. He asked, "About whom, pray, does the prophet say this, about himself or about someone else?" (Acts 8:34). Then, the deacon Philip "beginning with this scripture" interpreted this passage for him and "told him of the good news of Jesus" (Acts 8:35). As Christians, our reading of these Servant Songs (and especially the fourth one) is indelibly—and rightly—shaped by the fact that we hear these verses within the Palm Sunday and Good Friday liturgies. In doing so, we share in a long Christian tradition (going back to the Acts of the Apostles and the Church fathers) which saw in these passages a way to make sense of the scandal of the ignominious suffering and death of Jesus: Jesus is the servant who suffers and is exalted.

But, if any text has "a surplus of meaning," it is certainly these poems. Our Christian reading, which arises out of a certain specific hermeneutical starting point, cannot exhaust their richness. For the people to whom Second Isaiah was speaking these texts certainly had some level of meaning (other than pointing to a figure to come some five hundred years hence). Thus, in their day, they would rightly have asked, "*Who* is the servant?" Some have made a case that Second Isaiah was speaking of a figure from the past (Moses, Jeremiah, Zerubbabal); others have seen the portrait as an autobiographical description of the prophet himself; still others have argued for a collective understanding, so that the servant is Israel as a whole, or a specific segment of the righteous. If we concentrate on the final song for a moment, it quickly becomes apparent that the identity of the servant is not the only question; the text is equally ambiguous about the identity of the other key figures, for example, 52:15, "*they* shall see," 53:1, "who will believe what *we* have heard?" It is not clear exactly what the servant suffered (illness, imprisonment, persecution). Scholars cannot even agree if the servant actually died (each phrase in 53:8-9 can be translated and interpreted so that the servant does not physically die). With all these unanswered questions, we can either condemn the poem as at best muddled or, at worst, a total failure in communication, *or* we can begin to wonder if the problem is not with our questions! Perhaps the deepest, the "true" message of this poem will not come in the unravelling of all these details, nor even in sorting out the true identity of the key figure. For our purposes here, I suggest that we can look at these poems from a slightly different perspective.

What is clear is that the servant suffers. The way that the figure is described in popular language, "the Suffering Servant," aptly captures this one essential element, even though the terminology "suffering servant" is not inclusive of all that the servant does, nor is it even a biblical expression. The poet draws upon traditional language to describe the Servant's suffering; almost every word and motif can be paralleled from the Psalter (e.g. the specific word for pains Ps 38:17, 69:29, Job 33:19; despised and rejected Ps 22:6, 22:24, 119:22; in silence Ps 38:13, Jer 11:19). Clearly these verses are not a medical report, seeking to give a clinically accurate description of his condition. They are repetitious, circular, cumulative, but by this very fact they overwhelm us with the sense of suffering, shame, ignominy, and despair; this is clearly "a man of sorrows and acquainted with grief" (53:3).

The "we" who see the servant react in the expected way, "we esteemed him not" (53:3). In accordance with standard Old Testament thinking, suffering such as this is assumed to be a mark of divine displeasure. In a worldview which judged success, prosperity and long life as the marks of divine presence and favor, those who see the servant are, like Job's friends, models of orthodoxy in their reaction: "Yet we esteemed him stricken, smitten by God, and afflicted" (53:4). A person suffering so terribly that he seems no longer human (52:14) could rightly be counted as naught; surely God must be absent from such a person.

But then, something changes. The reader is not told exactly what, but the "we" suddenly discover that things are not as they seem. One of the most important words in the whole poem in the Hebrew is the little adversative *waw* which begins 53:10, "*yet* it was the will of the Lord to bruise him." The truth is that God has not been absent but, in some way, has been present to this suffering figure. In words which seem almost blasphemous, it was "the Lord" who "has laid on him the iniquity of us all" (53:6). The servant himself confesses that when "I gave my back to the smiters, and my cheeks to those who pulled out the beard" (50:6), even then the God "who vindicates me is near" (50:8). And in the end, God, who has been present in the depths of suffering, will also be present so that the suffering one "shall be exalted and lifted up" (52:13). The language of exaltation, like the language of suffering, is couched in terms which are traditional and somewhat vague; we are told only that the Servant will "see his offspring," "prolong his days," "be satisfied," "divide the spoil with the strong" (53:10-12).

Without reducing the poem to a simple allegory, there is obviously some relationship between Israel's experience of exile and the servant. To a people who knew rejection, the scorn of the nations, unimaginable suffering, Second Isaiah speaks with the conviction that all this is not happening apart from the Lord: God is present, even in their suffering. Ultimately the situation will be reversed; the nations who now surround Israel in power and mock them will one day stand in silent awe "for that which has not been told them they shall see, and that which they have not heard they shall understand" (52:15).

Our poem does not explain the mystery of suffering. It gives no easy answers about why this one should be "wounded for our transgressions" (53:5), nor does it lay out a theology of vicarious suffering to explain how "with his stripes we are healed" (53:5). All we know is that God is not absent from either this suffering or the final vindication. The servant who "will startle many nations" (52:15) still startles and astonishes us. Somehow, in this figure, oppressed and afflicted, "despised and rejected" (53:3), with "no form or comeliness that we should look at him" (53:2), we can recognize the presence of our God, a God "of sorrows and acquainted with grief."

"A Self-Hiding God" (Isa 45:15)

We have already considered a number of prophetic texts in which the language and image of God hiding his face is linked to human sinfulness, texts in which God's perceived absence is explicitly understood as an expression of judgement (pp. 168-170). But there is another sense in which we can talk of God as hidden: God (or the face of God) is hidden precisely because of what it means to be God.

Let us take as our starting point, a short but profound text from Isa 45:15:

> Truly, you are a God who hides yourself
> O God of Israel, the Savior.

Beginning at verse 14, Second Isaiah depicts a vision of the glorious future in which all the nations of the world (the Egyptians, the Ethiopians, the Sabeans) will come to acknowledge the uniqueness of the God of Israel and the presence of this God to his people; they will confess "God is with you only, and there is no other, no god besides him" (45:14). But immediately following this full and magnificent confession of faith on the part of the nations, it is, paradoxically, the prophet who acknowledges that this same God is a God "who hides yourself." The God who is present is also absent, hidden—yet, not totally hidden, or the prophet could not go on to - acknowledge this God as "the Savior." This is the paradox of a God known as Savior and yet still unknown and beyond human comprehension.

Often, this phrase in Isaiah is translated slightly differently, and so we talk of "the hidden God" (*deus absconditus* as the phrase has come to us from the Latin). Yet, the passive form "hidden" is not quite accurate. In Hebrew, it is the reflexive form of the verb which is used, an active verb of positive determination; perhaps this word would be better translated "a self-hiding" or "a self-concealing" God. Even in hiding, God acts with divine freedom and sovereignty. It is interesting to look at how the New English Bible has translated this verse: "How then can you be a god that hide yourself, O God of Israel, the deliverer?" But this is too facile a solution to a profound mystery; by using the form of a rhetorical question which calls forth a negative answer ("No, the God who delivers does not hide himself"), this translation simply dissolves the tension.

We have seen that throughout the Old Testament there is a living sense of a God who is truly holy, other, not able to be compared to anything known from the realm of human experience ("To whom then will you liken God, or what likeness compare with him?" Isa 40:18, "I am God and there is none like me" Isa 46:9). Using another image, the prophet tries again to express this sense of transcendence: "For my thoughts are not your thoughts, neither are your ways my ways, says the Lord. For as the heavens are higher than the earth, so are my ways higher than your ways and my thoughts than your thoughts" (Isa 55:8-9). Above all, in the experience of the exilic community, these words had become a living reality.

Yet, this confession of a hidden God is a confession of faith, not a lament. The incomprehensibility of God is a corollary of divine transcendence. The God who is Other cannot be circumscribed by any human concept, word or image. In the texts we are considering now, this situation is not blamed on human sinfulness or skepticism and doubt. It is not even a problem to be solved by repentance or by a willed act of faith. The God who is Other and conceptually inaccessible will always be hidden; even the God who is known and confessed as Savior is still ultimately hidden. A God who is totally accessible to finite human beings would, by definition, not be God. Or, as Paschal expressed it, "A religion that does not affirm that God is hidden is not true" (Pensées 586).

The insight of this prophetic confession of faith, "Truly you are a God who hides yourself," is foundational to any true Christian spirituality. While we as Christians acknowledge with grateful praise the richness and fullness of the revelation granted to us in Jesus Christ, our God too is a God who dwells in "unapproachable light" (1 Tim 6:16). After all our study of the gospels, after all our theological reflection and scholarly precision, we are driven ultimately to turn to the language of doxology. In words which could have been spoken by the exiles in Babylon, we confess,

> O the depths of the riches and wisdom and knowledge of God!
> How unsearchable are his judgements
> and how inscrutable his ways!
>
> (Romans 11:33)

BIBLICAL INDEX

[References and page numbers in bold print indicate extended discussions of the text; specific citations within these sections are not indicated]

SUBJECT INDEX